ACTION MANIFESTO OF A MADMAN FOR GOOD

BY: JAY SHERMAN

ACTION MANIFESTO OF A MADMAN FOR GOOD

©2013 lulu, all rights reserved

Unrelenting positivity

Author: Jay Sherman

ISBN: 978-0-578-12762-0

I DEDICATE THIS THIRD INSTALLMENT OF MY MANIFESTO TO ALL THE PEOPLE THAT HAVE FOUGHT AND STRUGGLED TO MAKE THE WORLD A BETTER PLACE. WE WILL GET PAST ALL OUR HITORICAL AND GENERATIONAL CHALLENGES WHEN WE ALLOW OURSELVES TO.

ACTION MANIFESTO OF A MADMAN FOR GOOD

ACKNOWLEDGMENTS

Thank you mom for always being there for me when I needed a kind word, and motivation that I'm good enough to achieve what is for my highest good; these books would not have been possible without you. To Pebbles for being a shining light in me and my mom's lives, you have shown us that love for people around us, is the only thing that really matters.

To Dad for always pushing me to achieve more than I thought possible, and for believing in me, even when I didn't believe in myself. To Grandma Yona for giving me culture at a young age so I never forget where I came from, and for great recipes that I am constantly making better. To Grandpa Herman for your unbelievable courage in overcoming enormous tragedy to have a life free of persecution and violence; you've shown the real importance of what it means to live in freedom.

To Grandma Laurine for being a pillar of strength and for proving that no matter what form love comes in, we can always count on it being there from the people we love and that love us. To Grandpa Mel for showing me that fishing out of an old van while drinking warm soda is great, especially when you're 10 and you're with your grandpa, every time I think about it, it makes me smile. I only hope I can create the same happy memories for my grandkids one day.

To Ryan for always being there to push my buttons, but at the same time being there with a cold beer and a friendly ear when I needed one, it means a lot. To Kendall for being in Ryan's life, you have helped him grow into an even better person. And for being there for me as well with a smile and an intelligent conversation, I only hope that I can find a wonderful woman that is the whole package just like you.

To Jess for being the beautiful and intelligent person you are, and for always believing in what I'm trying to accomplish; when the world changes for the better, it will be because of wonderful and caring people like you that "get it". To Sean for proving to me not only the importance of reveling in one's culture, but also experiencing other ones. We can make this world a better place brother, and we will. To April and Zeb for proving to me that when two people are there for each other 100%, they change the world around them for the better by making everything brighter; thank you for being a great example of how we can all be to each other. To Bob for providing the best space for a BBQ and some of the happiest memories I have, but also for showing that somebody can have some wild and crazy times, but can also have a brain in their head and care about what's going on around them.

To Mackey for being my greatest inspiration that I can achieve anything if I put my mind to it, and for proving that people don't have to walk the path created by their parents, but they can carve out a new one. To Tim for always being my buddy, and even though we might not see each other that much, our brotherhood never dims. To Laurie for opening my mind and heart to the way the world really is, this book series and passion for justice would surely not be as strong as it is if not for you. To Jaime for proving that no matter what cards one is dealt, we can achieve what is best for our souls when we pay attention to what's around us. When the world improves, it will be because of people like you that always keep their eyes and their minds open. To Pablo for always providing me with a laugh and an intelligent conversation; you have proven that anybody can move forward, they just need the will, and their path will open up for them.

To Brooke for always being there with a smile, a laugh and for being one of the most genuine people I know; and even though you might be the captain, and I am the admiral, we are both the best, even if we are on opposite teams.

To Lisa for providing a space where I can prove to myself, that money is not nearly important as being happy and striving towards what makes us happy, I am forever grateful. To Kayleen for being the sister I never had, and for never letting me talk bad about myself; you have proven time and time again that we love not because we want to, but because we have to.

To Doug for being the bag daddiest of them all, and for knowing that even though we have a long struggle ahead to help us evolve, we can make it if we keep our eyes and our heads on what's really important; when the next revolution comes, I want you by my side. To Marshall for always being there with a joke and a funny video, and for proving that life only has to be as serious as we make it out to be. To Cash who always wanted to see his name in a book ☺

To Aaron for genuinely caring about what I have to say, but also caring the how the world treats others. You surely "get" how we're all equal and all deserve to be happy, no matter what path we take in life or who we love. To Kathea for being able to keep up with the guys, and for proving that women can do anything a man can do if given the opportunity.

To Randy for all the great conversations, not only have you made many of my days brighter, but have proven to me that there are conscious people everywhere, we just have to look around. To Dale for always being there with a smile and a laugh; and don't worry, not only will the cookies keep coming, but when I accept my Pulitzer, it will be because of people like you that made me feel good about what I'm trying to accomplish. To Lee for proving that people with opposite opinions can find common ground, they can even come together and solve problems if they listen to what the other side has to say. To Randall for proving that people can make other's lives better by truly listening, and thank you for making the world a better place by spreading light and love.

To Aimee for showing me the more confidence that I have in myself, the more I will succeed; and for showing me it doesn't matter what anybody else thinks, only what makes us happy. To Mark and Linda for not only believing in what I am trying to accomplish, but also for being the greatest example I know of how when people are down to earth and honest about what they want, the world opens up to them.

To Mr. Calkins, Mr. Horak, Mr. Estrada and Mr. Melton for being some of the greatest teachers I had while going through school. Even though you are not on this earth anymore, I just want you to know how much of an impact you made on my life. You are the reason that I have had the courage and confidence to come out with this third book, and show the world that we can all achieve our goals, if we only critically think about our actions before we take them.

To Mr. Soderholm for being my first great teacher; junior high was tough sometimes, but you proved that laughing, having a good time but also thinking critically about what's around us, is how we get to where we want to go. To Mrs. Burstiner for instilling in me the want to uncover what the powerful sweep under the rug, and for proving that holding those in power accountable, is the only way we can evolve, because we are holding ourselves accountable at the same time.

To the 4th street market guy for all the great shirts, the words of wisdom when I come in to purchase mind altering substances, and for the great conscious conversations on how to fix the world. You are what every corner market guy should strive to be. To Matt Rivers for being there on that street corner that one day. If I wouldn't have walked down that street at that moment, I might never have heard your music, and I might never know how powerful it is to put as many conscious thoughts out there as we can for the whole world to pull from. And even though I might not ever come into contact with you again, I just wanted you to know that you're a great inspiration to me with your songs and your words, you have proven to me that we can all change the world, we just have to get out there and do it.

To the checkers at the COOP, thanks for always providing me with a smile, conversation and some down to earth vibes as I start my day. To the Marsh for being my Walden Pond, my refuge and the place that has been such a peaceful place that welcomes me any time I want. You have shown me so many forms of beauty, that even when I am somewhere else, I am right back there because I have had a glimpse of what the world is really like. May you always be there so other generations can see that once they glimpse the real beauty of the world, they will always be able to pull from it; that is the motivation that will help them strive to make the world a better place so we can collectively move forward as a species.

Thank you to the world, to the people I haven't met yet, and the people that are in my life now that make me want to be a better person. Sometimes I may get down in life feeling like I can't accomplish something, I'm just not good enough or maybe that something is meant for somebody else. What keeps me going is the thought that I can overcome and achieve because we can all overcome and achieve. We will get to where we need to go once we realize that peace, justice, humanity, accountability, equality and love is universal among us and what we need.

Love is the fuel for our gas tank of collective evolution. Will we keep refilling it as often as we need, or will we allow siphon hoses to come from all directions?

Thank you to my life for proving that no matter who you are, where you come from or what you believe, we all deserve to be happy. We can help our species and earth collectively evolve if we just allow ourselves to.

ACTION MANIFESTO OF A MADMAN FOR GOOD

INTRO

What do we do when there is nothing we can do; we do something we're passionate about. We get into this funk sometimes when it appears that the world's problems are too big and the powerful seem to gain more influence with each passing day; this is when we have to do something that makes us happy. If we are a reader we should pick up a book. If we are a writer, we should pick up a pen. If we enjoy the outdoors we should take a walk in nature. The point is to do something for ourselves that makes our souls sing.

Once our anxiety level has gone down, and our positive energy level has gone up, we will see things a bit differently; we will see the world's problems as not too big to solve because we can think clearly and openly about them. Most importantly, we will see the control that the powerful parade in front of our faces as the illusion it really is.

We will realize there are many more of us than there are of them. We will realize it is us that make the whole system function if we stand up and say we want to control our own lives; and we will never back down.

No more will we allow banks to leverage mortgages and value our home at less than we paid, because we will point out the falsities in increasingly large numbers. No more will we allow oil and chemical companies to dictate how we travel and what we eat, because we realize we are the ones that are buying all their crap. If we want solar, wind and biomass, not to mention safe food to eat, we will demand it.

If the big pharmaceutical companies keep their rates so high that the only quality health care goes to the super rich, we will stand up and demand that prices go down; and if the reason they keep them high is keeping their citizenry unhealthy and weak, we will expose that too.

If the military gets into another unjust war, or attacks and destroys a village with dozens or even hundreds of innocent people in it because one bad person "might" be heading there, we must stand up and demand that they do their homework so they can find the right answer like we had to in high school.

The point is being thankful for what we have so we can achieve more, the more of us that believe we can make positive change, the more of us that will. Our numbers will grow so large with critical thinking and universal human truth that the whole system designed to make us blind, dumb and full will fall apart; similar to how advertisements go away when we don't pay attention or put our faith in them, so too will a tyrannical governmental and corporate system.

What will emerge is a society that works and does what's best for all its inhabitants. Injustice, racism, evil and all bad energy will become so insignificant, that we will laugh at what a distant memory it is. We have the power. We have always had the power. We must open our eyes, minds and our hearts and get to work. Like the old saying that goes, "doing what we love is like being on vacation everyday", when we start bringing humanity, accountability and truth to ourselves so all of us achieve our dreams, it will be like second nature to us. We will wonder how we ever got along before.

ACTION MANIFESTO OF A MADMAN FOR GOOD

ENTRY#201

Have we ever found ourselves saying, why is the military fighting another war for murky purposes? Why are their goals stuck in the grey area? Are a fighter's goals ever crystal clear? If they were clear, would it even be called war? Or do soldiers really have honest and true goals, just not ones that are released to the public?

It's hard to not get angry when we hear about another country being attacked because of "terrorists", when really it's for resources and control of those resources. It's hard not to get angry when a country is full of gems, minerals or some other valuable mineable material, yet the majority of the country is extremely poor because foreign governments and corporations control all the extraction and sales.

The idea is to get past the anger, and look at it as taking in information. When we hear about a terrible military event, we might get upset and want to take violent action. We must get past this, so we can think rationally and clearly about what will authentically make the change we seek.

ACTION MANIFESTO OF A MADMAN FOR GOOD

ENTRY#202

If the military has a million methods to kill a person, how many methods do they have to build a person up? If they teach in boot camp how to use weapons, how to use strategy to eliminate the enemy and how to use what's around to one's advantage, do they teach the best ways to reach somebody and help them be all they can be is to teach them to think for themselves?

Critical thinking helps out in all aspects of life, especially war fighting. When we are given the tools to become better people, we can give them to others. We do need a national defense; if we are attacked we do need to be able to defend ourselves. But, if we aren't taught how to build up and only how to destroy, it will lead to our physical and spiritual ruin.

The sooner we learn the methods of peace that create a just and equal society, the sooner we can carry them out.

ACTION MANIFESTO OF A MADMAN FOR GOOD

ENTRY#203

There are always answers to life's most difficult questions, how much we pay attention will determine the quickness of the answer. If we see that a 20 year old private mowed down some innocent people amidst war because adrenaline took over, we must ask why they weren't given the tools to deal with their emotions. Did they think they had the right tools, but it was actually an identical concept designed for all soldiers, not something that was tailored to each soldier's emotional state? If they were given the special attention they sought and problems were found but stuck around anyway, we must ask ourselves if putting emotionally disturbed or emotionally broken people to the task of building people up will ever have a positive effect.

I realize it takes a certain disconnect with humanity to enter a theatre of war. But if we expect broken people to fix other broken people, our goals are completely backwards. We must fix ourselves if we are to fix others. We must ask the difficult questions, we must also listen and hear the answers.

ACTION MANIFESTO OF A MADMAN FOR GOOD

ENTRY#204

We want a better world, right? Does fighting for peace sound like loving war or loving hate? Does the fact that because bombs and missiles are so powerful these days that it makes some want the power to destroy the world, help us rest easier at night knowing annihilation could come at the flick of a button? Do we deserve the power to play God? Is the idea that one of us could control the world by fear cause the rest of us to cower and submit?

Those of us who talk about how the rapture will clear the world of all non-believers so it can be created anew are no different from those who want to build up their nuclear arsenals to 500 warheads because their neighbor has 499. We must demand on a daily basis and in all our actions that we want to live on a non-radioactive planet that actually sustains life. We must stand up for peace and humanity. If the world's destroyers are ready, so to must the world's creators. We can create or destroy, it is up to us. We must pay attention, so as to not get caught up by the double speak, on either side.

ACTION MANIFESTO OF A MADMAN FOR GOOD

ENTRY#205

Is it ever possible for a military victory to be guaranteed 100%? Is it even possible to determine? Does any side truly win when both sides suffer terrible and tragic losses? Where does the mentality come from that thinks we can take somebody over by force and they will love and respect us later for it?

If there is anything I've learned in life, it's that nothing is guaranteed, no matter how set in stone it might seem. If the war makers, war machine or military industrial complex believe so much in themselves that they attempt to take over war fighting and make it a private business (even if their actions guarantee mutual assured destruction), we must stand up and say enough is enough.

We must always stand up and point out when we see wrongs; we must write letters to our politicians and NGO'S, protest, rabble-rouse, whatever it takes to change a leaders thinking. But before we can change their idea that big explosions equal big victories, we must ask ourselves does that way of thinking only exist because we put our faith in it?

ACTION MANIFESTO OF A MADMAN FOR GOOD

ENTRY#206

If we believe we must stand up and fight, or flounder around knowing a problem exists but not knowing what to do, do we also believe that every question has an answer? Are there answers to all questions, or only to the right questions?

Sometimes we can get caught up on words like fighting, standing up, respect, humanism, accountability and think that the words themselves are the end all be all for problem solving. While words aid in the solution, they are only part. The other part is planning and action. The point is we have to integrate all these ideas because they don't work against each other, they work off of each other. We must have thoughts, then words, ideas, plans and then actions.

While it is true that nothing would happen without positive action, action wouldn't even be possible without words, ideas and plans. We must think about positive change, and then work to make it a reality. We have to think about what we want before we can make it happen.

ACTION MANIFESTO OF A MADMAN FOR GOOD

ENTRY#207

If we think about life's repercussions of our actions, does that change our actions? If we weigh the pros and cons of going to war, defending our way of life or standing up to a devilishly corrupt and morally bankrupt government and corporate system, will it guarantee a more positive outcome?

When we are looking for solutions to ingrained historical and generational problems, do we look at their root causes and functions? Do we look at ourselves and our own lives so we can correlate and make sense of problems before they appear en-masse with a much more influential footing?

Just as a politician has to weigh every word they say for its possible impact, so must we. If a military or a "private security company" shoots first and asks questions later, is it because that's how we go through our daily lives? Can we change their way of thinking if we change our way of thinking?

ACTION MANIFESTO OF A MADMAN FOR GOOD

ENTRY#208

Are drones and attacking people anonymously the future of warfare? Will we no longer put large numbers of soldiers on the ground because we don't want to risk the lives of our own? Do we think we can get in and get out a lot quicker if we rain death from above? Are we living the future that Eisenhower talked about when he warned about the military industrial complex, or is this a future that he didn't envision?

The idea of a military industrial complex is when private business takes over war fighting functions, supply and manufacturing so that it's done for profit; which could help describe our present situation because we definitely fight for resources and private companies definitely make drones and even operate them in some instances. My big question is, if President Eisenhower was warning about war profiteering, wasn't he also arguing for smaller and more specialized units to go into fight? He wasn't against war and going in some place, he just wanted to do it on a smaller scale with more surgical attacks, get in and get out. Isn't that what we are attempting to do now? Does this issue go to the heart of war itself?

ACTION MANIFESTO OF A MADMAN FOR GOOD

ENTRY#209

Unjust wars and corrupt practices seem to be a symptom of a much bigger societal issue. Are power struggles, resource battles, and ethnic cleansing reasons and causes of war because we ourselves do it in our everyday lives? Do we have to change ourselves before we can change the system?

If we want to stop unjust wars, we must stop thinking any war is just. If we want to stop corrupt practices, we must stop thinking that corruption is a result of actions taken, but something that is in the heart of the system, causing the actions to happen in the first place.

We must try not to fight with our neighbor for any reason, not try to take advantage of them so we can have a leg up on what society thinks we should be. We should not believe that all of our problems spring out of thin air. The issues we deal with on a daily basis only magnify when we attain a certain office or position. War and corruption exists in political and business leaders because it exists in us. We must help ourselves so we can help the world.

ACTION MANIFESTO OF A MADMAN FOR GOOD

ENTRY#210

If we created the mentality that spurned military and corporate supremacy in the first place, is there an easy answer for fixing it? If all of us create our own reality by integrating our thoughts and feelings into the actions we take because of life experience, is it possible that we can ever be told by some outside source about a solution that will work for us? If we learn differently, do we react differently as well?

The answer to fixing our psyche, so we can fix societal problems so we can fix our politics and military, is unique to every person; everybody will come up with a different solution that will work for them. What we must never forget is the idea that at the basic root level, we are all the same. We all come from different backgrounds, areas, ethnicities, races, religions and sexual orientations, but what makes us human is exactly the same.

To find the answers we seek we must see that we are different and the same simultaneously, for balance is the way to sustain life. Do we want to destroy each other or create together?

ACTION MANIFESTO OF A MADMAN FOR GOOD

ENTRY#211

If the healthcare system is broken, and it looks like there is no way to fix it, how do we find a solution? I guess the first questions to ask are, how is it broken and who is benefiting because it is broken?

If prices keep rising for copays, visits, tests and meds, and insurance seems to cover less and less, we should demand to know why. When the price is raised for a visit or copay, who decides on it, the doctor, insurance company, government agency, etc.....?

The whole system seems to work off of itself. It's structured in a way that makes it impossible to tell where the change is coming from. It's designed to keep us from knowing what the people at the top are really up to. Just like the answer to most things, follow the money and you can usually find how and why things happen.

And all this happens if you already have insurance, what happens when you don't have any?

ACTION MANIFESTO OF A MADMAN FOR GOOD

ENTRY#212

We can wait and wait for the answers to come, but what if they don't? Does it mean that they're not out there? Does it mean that the answers are out there, but they're only meant for somebody with higher intelligence, a bigger house, a better job, a nicer car and the trophy spouse? Or are we just not finding the answers we seek because we are not actually seeking them, but waiting for them to fall into our laps?

We must be vigilant and courageous in chasing after our passion, which will provide a path to the answers we seek. Once we find it, we must learn how to grow within it. There are a lot of messages in society that say we can't do something, but they're wrong. Let's get off our asses and take action to fix what we all agree needs fixing. We will come together, we will fight the powers that be, but we must find our own path, our own trail to the treasure. The treasure being enlightenment, and the trail being treating each other humanely and lovingly so we can fight the battles that are actually worth our time!!!

ACTION MANIFESTO OF A MADMAN FOR GOOD

ENTRY#213

To find out what actions are worth our time and blood and sweat, we must look inside ourselves. We must look into the deepest darkest depths of our soul to see what we might be scared to admit. We must find what makes us happy, what brings us up when we are feeling down, what gives us energy when we are feeling drained and what will motivate us to overcome obstacles and break out of the chains we have put on ourselves.

Once we find out what drives us, then we will have the energy and the will to carry on. Once we have built this up inside of ourselves and are able to use it in the front of our minds instead of the back, the answers will become much clearer. The actions we must take will become so obvious to us, that there will be nothing else to do, we must act.

Taking down and/or restructuring a multi-generational system meant to protect the powerful and subvert and control the rest isn't going to be easy. But it is 100% impossible if we don't even make the attempt.

ACTION MANIFESTO OF A MADMAN FOR GOOD

ENTRY#214

When one of us pops up with the old line, "well, we all want to take action, but what do we do" somebody might pop up and say, "well if we only did this, this and this then we would be on our way". I guess it doesn't always happen that way, but it seems like a majority of the time when we are around our friends, family or somebody of like mind, it comes to this. Everybody agrees on the problem, and everybody agrees on the solution and that's it, it doesn't seem to go any further. It's as though talking about it and even saying what we would do is enough. That just because we vocalized it, somehow these words will carry on to somebody who will do something.

We can break out of this mold by realizing, discussing and talking back and forth about what is important, but it's only the first of many steps. The next is to take those actions that we all seem to agree on anyway, and get out and do them.

Talk is cheap, but it's completely free and meaningless if it's not backed up by action.

ACTION MANIFESTO OF A MADMAN FOR GOOD

ENTRY#215

Actions that we dream about and then talk about must only be taken if we are ready. The worst thing we can do is try to go out and change the world when we don't believe in our hearts that it's possible. We must stay positive and believe that things will work out if we put our full faith in the process, and act towards the betterment of everybody.

Sometimes I even ask myself if this huge undertaking that I have started is worth it. Can I even accomplish the things that are burning and churning within my soul, calling me to act? The answer is I can because I keep going, and I keep moving forward.

If MLK said the universe bends towards justice, then it will bend towards the right and not toward the wrong. The thing is, it only bends towards justice when we do the bending, when we do the hard work required. Positive change will happen for all of us when all of us work towards it. Once we realize this, we can come together, and then we can act. We will be ready for action when we can't see any other solution other than to uplift and care for ourselves so we can uplift and care for others; positivity is a very reciprocal quality.

ACTION MANIFESTO OF A MADMAN FOR GOOD

ENTRY#216

So much rage, so much pain, it's hard to know where to start. There can be so much darkness sometimes that the light has no way to shine through. The whole misinterpreted thing about it is that the darkness is an illusion. Sometimes it's an illusion of our own making, sometimes the chains and blocks that we find impeding ourselves from the truth, are put on by ourselves to keep us from moving forward, to keep us from evolving. Sometimes we believe they are the most comfortable because we know exactly what they're about, even though in actuality they're making us very uncomfortable. But we know them and therefore they are less scary than the big dark unknown.

What we all need to realize is that yes, what's out there can be scary and anxiety filled because it is unknown. But, it also can be totally exciting, meaningful and for our highest good.

We need to try to flip around the way we think so we can achieve our dreams. Nobody will accomplish our goals for us, only we have the ability to go out there and get what we truly want and need.

ACTION MANIFESTO OF A MADMAN FOR GOOD

ENTRY#217

Once we start changing around the way we think, we will start looking at everything in a different way. Everything will seem a little bit different, that's because it will be. If we start looking at the world from a more open and aware of "what's around us" perspective, then things start to not be so scary and intimidating. Events that used to scare us, we will welcome. Because although they have the potential to do us physical and emotional harm, they also have the ability to give us the strength to achieve the things we only dreamed about.

We start flipping the way we think by asking ourselves one little question, where would we like to end up in life, what would we like to achieve, what would bring our soul the most joy? We must ask ourselves what we truly think, not what somebody else thinks, and because they aren't truly in our head, they can't put us down; the only one that can put us down, is us.

We have to stop beating ourselves up over petty crap, because if we can't treat ourselves with respect, then how can we expect anybody else to. We must remember to always love ourselves first, so we can love others. We need to find out what our souls need, so we can help others make discoveries as well. We have the power if we choose to accept it.

ACTION MANIFESTO OF A MADMAN FOR GOOD

ENTRY#218

It's a matter of choice to accept the power that we can make positive change, not some outside energy force. It's not some overarching power structure that is sucking the life out of us. It's not the system or the politicians that make us feel bad or guilty or like less of a human being for wanting to make life better for everybody, not just for us and people we know.

There are so many things in the world that could use fixing. So many ingrained historical and generational issues, it's hard to know where to start. The important factor is not where we start, when or how quickly we start, or how quickly we finish. The only important thing is that we do start. We must start now.

Like the old saying goes, even when we haven't decided, we still have made a choice. We can choose to make a difference or not to. Does any of it matter, only if we think it does? Change starts from within us, it's not created or introduced later, it grows through heart ache and pain, but also love and understanding. We must make the right choice. The faith of humanity rests in our hearts.

ACTION MANIFESTO OF A MADMAN FOR GOOD

ENTRY#219

I don't know if I'm just growing more cynical as I get older, or if the world is just getting farther and farther away from the light. If it's within me, and all choice and action stems from what I think, what do I do? How can I change the world if I can't even change myself? How can I make somebody believe in the faith of humanity, if I don't believe in it myself?

The truth is I do have faith in humanity, in the basic goodness of people. Now not everybody is good, not everybody that we run into out there on the street will want to do something good for us or to us. Some of them might even want to do us harm. We have to be open and vigilant to whatever is in front of us. If we don't, life will just run us over and take whatever is not nailed down.

When we open ourselves up to all of life's possibilities, we really open up our soul; when we allow outside influences into our routine, we must stay vigilant. They could be out to do us harm, or they could be out to do for us what we might not be able to for ourselves. This is part of the way the universe can correct itself.

We will be much better off and so will the world, if we are kind and nurturing to ourselves. It's hard sometimes to be motivated if we have always told ourselves how much we suck, and how we will never be able to accomplish our dreams. This is part of flipping the conversation. If we tell ourselves we can accomplish something, we can, and that's all that matters. If we believe in ourselves, then so will others, just like the cycle of life. With us in the driver's seat, we will be ready to take on the ideological battles that are holding back the world; that which are holding back our souls. We need to bust through the darkness and see how much light the world really has.

ACTION MANIFESTO OF A MADMAN FOR GOOD

ENTRY#220

The key to uniting people around things we already know we agree on, is realizing that it's the same basic things that drive all of us. We all want to make a decent living; we all want to take care of our families. We all want to accomplish something great in our lives that will affect major positive change somewhere on the earth, we want to be remembered.

Now, we all take different paths to get where we are going. They are different races, different religions, different cultures, different sexual orientations and different ways of thinking and looking at the world. The ties that bind us together are not what make us different; they're what make us the same. We might all be taking different paths, but we're all going after and towards the same basic thing, happiness and enlightenment.

All the different ways of getting to the light can make life more stressful and complex, but when you really sit down and look at it, it makes life more exciting and original. It's almost not worth getting out of bed in the morning if it's going to be the same old same old. Life is not scary because of all the problems out there to harm us, it is inviting because of all the opportunities to love and evolve.

Do we want to evolve? Do we as a people want to grow past this state that we have put ourselves in? Do we want to admit that we created evil minded politicians by being evil minded ourselves? If we want to make the world aware, we must start with looking in the mirror, and looking within ourselves. If we want to help unite people around a common goal, we must unite ourselves around a common thought of action. Let's go out there and create some positivity, because we know what will happen otherwise.

ACTION MANIFESTO OF A MADMAN FOR GOOD

ENTRY#221

If we are going to change the world by changing ourselves, we must start by changing our thought process. We must start by waking up in the morning and being thankful. Just the simple act of showing gratitude can be so rewarding and fulfilling because it came from us. Now I'm not talking about sitting down and praying, although if that's what makes sense for you and that's the path you are on, by all means go for it; lord knows I am the last person in the world to stop someone's stream of consciousness, no matter where it comes from or who it emanates from.

The first thing we should think of when we roll out of the bed in the morning is how lucky we are to be alive. There is always somebody out there in the world that has it worse than us. That although we might be going through extremely hard times, there is always somebody out there whose challenges are just a little more vivid. This might not always put a smile on our face, but it will help put things into perspective. If we can see how somebody could overcome something believed to be impossible, then our problems will pale in comparison.

A feeling of gratitude towards all things will change our energy levels. It will affect everything we do, and all the actions we take on any given day. When we have gratitude on our minds, we have love in our hearts. If we have love in our hearts, then we will have the power to make the major changes that will help all of us, not just some of us.

Starting from a place of gratitude changes the whole ball game. Do we want to be the one controlling our actions, or do we want to relinquish that to somebody else? Being thankful and showing gratitude brings up the whole idea that we have a choice. We always had free will, and we will always continue to have it as long as we never take it for granted. We must be thankful for it every day. Especially those days when we are down and feeling blue; if we can pick ourselves up and dust ourselves off, no obstacles under any circumstances ever have the chance to stop us. There is no greater power in the world than gratitude.

ACTION MANIFESTO OF A MADMAN FOR GOOD

ENTRY#222 AND BEYOND

I woke up this morning and was thankful, and the day just seemed a little brighter. I was excited to get out of bed and approach the day. The sun was out and I was going to get some writing done on this very book.

Then just because I was open and willing to take whatever the day brought, (and because the only way I was going to enter into it was with a warm feeling of gratitude) I have had a smile on my face all day.

This is the place we have to get to, where we are happy just to get up in the morning; because we know we're going to have new and fulfilling experiences that are the essence of what makes life worth getting out of bed. When we wake up with this gratitude, all the things that might have bothered us are put into perspective.

What we have to get at the store, what we have to fill our hearts with so we can carry on through the days challenges, what issues are holding back our human evolution, will all become less scary and stressful, and more introspective and rewarding when we're thankful.

We have to start our evolution from this place of introspection and consciousness, because it is the first step that will lead to the others. If we try to skip a stair walking up a staircase we might skip over something vitally important, such as what makes us walk the steps in the first place

These steps will also keep things in perspective. They are there to help and guide us, so as we are learning, we are experiencing at the same time; which is one of the most important parts, I can't stress it enough. We must experience what we learn as we learn it. We must touch and feel, and truly understand what we are inputting into our brains.

If we don't, we will learn about all the human processes and how people can fix those issues that are simple yet hard at the same time, but we will find ourselves in a quandary. We will know how the whole thing works, but because we never experienced it, we won't know exactly what it's like. We won't know what the process is actually about because we didn't input it into our heart and soul, only our minds; we didn't take it down the divine eighteen inches from our mind to our heart.

We will see the end game, and feel with every fiber of our being that we want to be there, yesterday. We will know what the end result should be, and have a relatively good idea of how sweet it will be when we get there. But, because we haven't experienced all the steps along the way as were learning how that common end goal can be achieved, we will want it to just happen and won't want to work for it.

We might think that because we know what it is, it might be good enough, or if we tell a few people who are like minded, then that might be enough. That we will just hope upon hope that things will work out. That just picturing the end game and getting other people to do the same, will be how ultimate enlightenment can be achieved. And although this is definitely part of it, being able to envision life when we all become more conscious happens when we pull our heads out of our asses, and really see the world around us as an important part of the process. But its only part, of which there are many.

I'm not saying I have all the answers, or how everything should be all the time. All I'm saying is that we can't just wait around for solutions to fall out of the sky, or come from somewhere else; we have to create them ourselves. This is where paying attention and taking the steps in order comes in. We get the ideas, talk about them, and start to unite around what we already know we agree on. Then we go out and take action together for the betterment of us all.

What happens if a step is skipped, and we can see the end game, but aren't sure how to get there? This is when we have to go back to the beginning, and start again with the basics. We have to remember what drives people, what helps them to realize their passion for helping humanity evolve, and how we see each other in ourselves. Basically, we have to remember how to be good to people, and treat others like we would like to be treated.

I only bring all this up, because I am guilty of this myself, I have found myself having to work back from the beginning for several years now. I can see and feel how people can unite around the basic ideas of love and understanding, but failed to carry out conscious action in bringing it all into reality.

This doesn't mean I give up, by all means, heavens no. I can never give up. Even though some days, are really hard. Now I don't mean give up in the physical body sense, I just mean give up in the "trying to fix the world with solutions that everybody already knows about but might not be willing to admit" kind of sense.

I find myself getting depressed sometimes about not being further along in life then I should be, and how the state of the world just seems to be getting worse and worse with the same problems repeating themselves over and over and over again in multiple settings, with countless variables coming in from every imaginable angle.

It can be over whelming, it can make me tired and just want to sleep; because at least then I can have some peace and nobody will bother me, I can just be myself. But this isn't true, is it? We are still plagued with our thoughts as we go to sleep. The only time we are not, is when we numb our thinking abilities with any form of mind alteration. This is when we have to get back to basics, and start being aware of what's around us.

I've thought about why this is happening, and I think I have come up with a solution to it. I'm feeling depressed about the state of the world, of the environment, my life in general, because I'm not actively introducing ideas that I know in the deepest darkest depths of my soul will fix what needs to be fixed. I need to take action.

I have found a lot of depression stems from this feeling of not taking action. Of feeling like there is no way it could ever be better, so why should we try. This feeling is everywhere only because we allow it to be. We allow this feeling to lurk into our brains, and affect everything we do.

When we take action and are active participants in fixing or even attempting to fix the things we know how to fix, our whole attitude changes. We become lighter; a smile might even pop out on our faces. When was the last time we randomly smiled? That is an example of a simple action that can change somebody's whole way of being. Because if we can't even smile at each other as we go down the street, how can we ever expect to get past all the things we know we could get past if we were just human to each other. This is also where gratitude comes in, which is the ultimate positive that we can take first thing in the morning, and use continuously throughout the day causing everything to change.

If they say that everything in life is perspective, and the meanings of people and events can completely change depending on how we look at them, then being thankful is exactly what we need to get started.

I struggle with this, as I am sure many of us have that have attempted it. Like the old saying that goes something is easier said than done, being thankful can be one that definitely falls on the list. But, the difference is that we know it's easier said than done, and if we do it, if we take action, then we really see what we've been missing out on. What was making us depressed might have been something completely out of our control.

The tricky part is knowing when we have depressed ourselves, or somebody else has done it to us. Now, sometimes we can't help when somebody does something that affects us. Sometimes they try and even succeed in doing us harm. This is when we have to remember that we can't always change everything that happens but we can always change how we react. And by changing how we react to a situation, we change its inherent meaning. And by changing its meaning, we have changed the whole idea that gives the powerful their power in the first place. We are making a change on the outside, by making a change within ourselves.

When we make change within ourselves, we begin to see the world differently, just as when we are thankful and show gratitude for everything we have instead of being upset about what we don't. This is the whole idea behind critical mass and the whole idea of one person changing the world with a message.

When we believe we can make a change, we can. When we believe that what somebody else puts in front of us should be taken as the gospel and never questioned, is when we fall into a trap of putting ourselves down. We fill our heads with messages of how we will never succeed, how there is no chance of it happening, that I am only one person, so what can I do to possibly affect anything that's going on. The banks are controlling the world and its resources with the help of despotic governments and spy agencies, so how could we ever even hope to get past that unimaginable obstacle?

It starts by knowing and believing that despots and black operations power are just an illusion, that they don't really control things; we do, but relinquished control a long time ago. Whether it was because of fright, pressure, a want to be comfortable or to fit in, we acquiesced and said "okay, I won't try and fight you. You control the messages I see. You shape the world so you can sell me a whole bunch of worthless crap that blinds me to what's really going on, just so you can keep carrying out your nefarious dealings. The thing is, now we have woken up. We can see the power that you project, and see it as just that, a projection."

When somebody is projecting an attitude or feeling onto somebody (judging how they are, how they act and why they do the things they do), they are really just pointing out their own deficiencies and where they are lacking. There are weaknesses in the armor, because there is really no armor in the first place, we only think there is; again it's projection. It will only affect us if we let it.

ACTION MANIFESTO OF A MADMAN FOR GOOD

BEYOND

I often look into the unknown and get frightened. I get scared about what new problems will arise that I never saw coming, or ones I did see coming that I failed to do anything about. Sometimes all I see is empty space, a void that will swallow me up if it ever has the chance. But what makes me feel better when I'm down is that the unknown will only swallow me up if I let it. It will only get to me and change the light hearted and loving nature that bleeds from my soul, if I let it. The unknown will take every piece of proof a loving person ever existed, if we let it.

I know this might seem like I am painting this whole thing out like a battle. Like I am stepping onto a battlefield in the fight for my life, and if I don't succeed, than that's it and any memory of me will be wiped from the earth. Sometimes I picture a battlefield with all the fallen soldiers that died for what they believed in (or what they were forced to believe in), and I see the deeper meaning and the metaphor that corresponds to their life.

All those fallen bodies, all that blood and gore, is just energy and passion to make the world better, in their or their close friend's eyes; for better or worse, they gave their life. Now, there have been many people that have fallen in the great struggles for justice, rights and dignity. They fought with everything they had, and weren't able to carry out their full potential because it was cut short. It was extinguished before the full and true meaning could be realized.

What we should take away from all this is not a feeling of sadness that they didn't succeed, but warmth in our soul because they attempted to change something in the first place. An issue in their heart was so strong, they were willing, and so full of energy that they just needed to go out and take action. They went out with what weapons they had, whether it was a pen, a microphone or a gun, and fought for what they thought was right (or what they were forced to think was right). In this they found their real purpose in life. They figured out that we were all put on this earth to take action.

We weren't put here to just sit around and be complacent and apathetic to all the problems around us. We weren't put here to see somebody suffering, and just walk by them because what we have going on is way more important than whatever they happen to be complaining about. We weren't put here to only surround ourselves by wants and needs that satisfy us and the very close circle around us; we were put here to benefit society as a whole.

If we weren't put here to help other people, then why were we put here? Were we granted this amazingly precious and finite thing they call life and free will, just so we can squander it by deeply caring about something only if it personally affects us? Were we put on this earth to be robots that are operated by some outside source, controlling not only what we say and what we do, but most importantly what we think?

The answer is an unequivocal no. We weren't put here to only care about ourselves. We weren't put here so we could just stomp on whoever gets in our way of achieving what some huge corporate entity wants us to, just so we buy their product.

We were put here so we can better ourselves. What we have to realize (and this is crucially important), is that we better ourselves so we can better others, not so we can ignore them. Humans are social beings; we thrive on interaction with people that don't want to see us fail at every turn. We have to get past the anger. We have to get past the hate. We have to get past the way that every time a mass movement makes its way into the news, the only things that get talked about are what buildings were damaged, and how the marchers are radicals and anarchists, only looking to tear the system down.

We realize all that. We know all that stuff is happening. We have to not ignore that it's happening, but we must be conscious of what's going on, what we can expect, and what the actual problem is. The solution might be to follow the money; that the way to fix problems are to find out who it benefits, and who it affects. If we did this, it wouldn't immediately change the fact that rights movements are painted as anarchist troublemakers, but it would help us see that the more upset the people at the top get, the closer we are to getting at the root of the problem.

The people who control things and keep the system in line, get more upset, angry and vicious when there is enough of an upwelling of support to make them feel threatened; when they feel there iron grip is slipping. We must realize that this is when we have to hunker down and not run away. We must meet this rage with love; it's how we break this seemingly endless cycle. How we get to the point of love is how we evolve. How we evolve and get past our anger is by not ignoring it, but by recognizing it, taking away anything that can be useful, and then letting it go. The letting go part is the really important thing because, if we don't let it go and we always stay angry, it gives us a false sense of being.

If we stay open minded and clear headed, we will start to realize the things around us. We will start to see all the injustice in the world, how there are things we might have ignored, and how terribly people can treat each other. If we stay with anger, and try to act through it, our actions will not be clear. There is no possible way to think straight when we are angry. This passionate anger can drive us to action, (and action is a good thing) but if we aren't able to think clearly about what the implications and consequences of what we are about to do are, we probably shouldn't do it. We should probably slow down, think and ponder what is really going on, what the real issues are, and why we are acting and or fighting in the first place.

This slowing down period is of immense help when we are trying to design a plan of attack. Once we get past anger, we will still see from time to time things and events that are awful, terrible and more horrible than we could ever imagine. The difference will be this time, that instead of immediately flying into a rage, we will slow down and think and just see it as taking in information . We will be able to look at the cause and effect, and what the underlying issues are. We will begin to formulate a solution because we are looking at everything in the bigger sense. Everything affects everything else, and positive change starts with us; whether its rage or reason is up to us.

Accountability is a grand concept. The idea of acting without thinking can seem like second nature to us. When we have been conditioned in such a fast paced lifestyle that asks so much of us on a daily basis, sometimes the only way to survive is automatic pilot.

This is why we have to change our way of thinking, or better yet, just start thinking all together. There is definitely a concept that exists that can slow this whole thing down, and that is obsessing. There is such a thing as over analyzing that keeps us from ever forming actions, because we are always thinking of all the possibilities, which keep our minds spinning out of control. This is when we have to decide what our buttons and levers are that will get us to act. What will drive us so strongly and give us such a passionate feeling that the only option we have is to act?

When we think about the world around us, we see what we can change and what we can't. We see the atrocities that make our blood boil, and the genocide and hate that are bleeding the world dry of its humanity. We also see all the good in people taking care of each other, and all the love and understanding that help push forward our collective positive evolution as a species. This is again where balance comes in.

Balance is in important in all things. It's important so we know what is positive and what is negative, because they are the definition of balance. We wouldn't know what one was without the other. Without positive things happening, we wouldn't know what the negative things are and vice versa.

Somebody was running in a field, the sun was shining, the birds were chirping, and the day couldn't have been more perfect. Except the person running through the field is being chased by a gunman that is trying to kill them. Whether this scene happens in wartime or in civilian life is irrelevant; they both usually have the same end result, the loss of human life.

The point is an all-encompassing perspective. We could see the person running through the field as a metaphor for the part of us that has gotten so far away from nature, that as we attempt to capture even a small sliver of it, we're chased down by the force that wants not to recapture what is true nature, but what their physical re-creation of what they think nature should be. Only when making millions upon billions of dollars is it worth it to the people at the top, if they can make some bucks off of us collectively not getting back to nature, then they will build a damn strip mall everywhere and anywhere they damn well please.

They will squash anything and everything that gets in their way. They act out of profit motive and greed for themselves and their inner circle. They act with a clear set of goals of where they want to go, what consequences they can endure, and what payoffs, sacrifices and judgments they'll have to make is all part of their decision making process.

Now do they sometimes act without thinking, sure, they are only human just like us. They have the same needs and desires as us, they just might happen to have a giant amount of power and influence that helps them get anything they want (regardless if it is somebody else's, or many somebody else's).

So even though we might not have the same size bank accounts or the same size houses or cars, we are all human. We all have to go through the same process of taking in information, analyzing it, and trying to make sense of raw data we can articulate so people come over to our point of view. Consciousness and mindfullness are human things, no matter what income scale, class, race, creed, religion, gender, age or sexual orientation we come from, we all think. If we didn't think, we would just be walking around like robots all the time, just waiting for our next oil change and lube job.

If we were robots, we would be put forth on an assignment, and we would move forward without fully knowing why we're moving forward. We would go without thinking because all of our physical and material needs are being met. And if they aren't being met, the system plants the idea in our minds that if we don't have all the things we see our neighbor enjoying, then there must be something wrong with us, and we need to be striving towards those things that they have.

We have a much better chance of succeeding if we think about our actions before we make them. If we are very angry and/or passionate about something, (and a fire is burning within us that feels like it's going to explode if we don't do something) we want to make positive action as fast as possible. Sometimes a quick decision can be the difference between life and death, forcing us to act whether we want to or not; this is why we must think

If we can let any thought enter into our head, it would be a good thing. If we have a gut feeling that the action we are about to take might not be the right one, it should be listened to as it is our inner truth. The idea of knowing when to listen, when to ignore and when to follow what we know in our heart is the right thing to do is very important. This is a feeling that is so strong, that the very makeup of it permeates every corner of our soul. We know how we feel, we know how the world feels for the most part about it, and we know what the guy down the street would say, so we just do it. This is called unconsciousness because we act from previous thoughts we had. This can be hard for some to understand because it's not something learned over night, but through much training of our minds.

We can act without thinking, we can act with thinking, and we can act because of previous thought. Is there anything else that will cause us to go through another thought and action process? I don't know, I don't know everything; but, I am open to all of life's possibilities, and therefore love to hear what everybody has to say. If I am truly open to hearing everything, and keeping only what best serves me, I have to listen when others speak and give me their thoughts and opinions (even if I don't like them). This is definitely something that is learned over time.

We get to the point of hearing, then listening, and then talking. But before we can get to the point of talking, there might come a stage where there is screaming, yelling, name calling, insults and all matter of attempted back stabbing and slander being tossed about just to throw the other one off their game. This happens because there wasn't a convergence of basic thought and opinion.

I'm not talking about agreeing with what everybody says, I'm saying that when we hear people out, we find that all too often common ground gets overlooked because of political, social or religious reasons, or just because the person feels threatened by new ideas and a different outlook. To introduce a new way of thinking, can blow somebodies mind apart because it might be 180 degrees from their thinking. It could turn their world upside down to actually conceive that there is another way to think and be, a way that we can all come together like we never have before, but always knew deep down we could.

Sometimes I feel like I'm beating around the bush, like I am not coming to a conclusion that any sane human being could comprehend. Then I remember that there is a lot of other people out there just like me. People that feel so strongly in their hearts that they want to affect the positive evolution of the world, but they don't know what to do, or exactly where or in what form to do it.

I attempted to write this book as my action; as my putting something forward into the world that is conscious and forward thinking, but also completely relatable to anybody that is human and sees that there is something going on, or thinks that there has to be a way to change our trajectory away from spiritual death and empire collapse. Also and most importantly, I believe this book is relatable to everybody that is human because they are human, and as humans, the same basic things drive us.

The need for food, water, shelter and clothing of course is universal among us. We all strive for it, just in different ways and with different means because of where we live or because of how we live. The need to be social beings, the need to be accepted as human beings, the need to protect and take care of our family, to make sure our kids are raised right, the need to not struggle and be stuck in survival mode so we can really put our full spiritual attention forward is universal.

It has been a struggle to find the right words to fully describe what I feel in my heart is such an easy solution to such a long lasting problem. It's one of those things that's easy and hard at the same time. It's easy because there are basic things we have always known to be true, that get ignored for all sorts of reasons and events. It's hard because they get at the heart of who we are, why we act, and what we do with our daily lives that makes life worth living not only to us, but to the rest of the world as well.

The idea is to just be good to each other, to see ourselves in every person we interact with. What are their needs and concerns and how do they differ from ours, and do they differ from ours at all? Humanism is the idea of treating everybody like we would like to be treated. Would we like somebody to put us down for the religion we believe in even though we might believe in it very strongly and believe it's helping us find the light? So why do we do it to others?

Why do we put others down for their religion, when we wouldn't want to be put down for ours? Would we want somebody to put us down for what we look like, where we're from, or who our parents or family might be? The answer of course, is no. Instead of seeing everybody else's path as not righteous and only leading to hell (or somewhere not as good as ours), we should see it as just another path to the same place; another window to the same room, or another door to the same spot.

Just because somebody isn't exactly physically like us, doesn't mean they are so different, or will think completely out of the norm. All it means is that we all come from different places and ways of thinking and being. The idea is to find our similarities, not our differences. This is where the idea of the old poster that used to hang up a lot in the 80s "All I really needed to know I learned in kindergarten" comes in. It is true. If we could remember to treat others like we would like to be treated (play nice in the sandbox), and really carry that to the full extent of what it truly means, then we have won a major battle, or a better way to put it, we have come to a better understanding, an evolution if you will; be nice to each other in the sand box of life. Next up is accountability because it goes hand in hand with humanism and treating others like we would like to be treated.

Accountability is used in our society to keep people in line to their government and vice versa, keep in line to their spouses, teachers, guides and their employers. It can be used for many sinister purposes to keep people down, but it can also be used for making sure politicians aren't taking advantage of people and getting away with whatever they want.

This is how control seems so overpowering and all-encompassing. The politicians, big money funders and behind the scenes string pullers are trying to get away with as much as they can before they get caught. It is like a teenager getting caught sneaking out late, taking the car without permission, doing drugs or drinking, they are constantly testing their limits.

So is a politician, they are always and forever testing what they can get away with and what they can't. When they know they can get away with anything, (or should I say when they think they can get away with anything) their actions will get bolder until they get caught. They are getting away with it because we allow them too. We allow them to pass laws that only benefit themselves and their friends, while squashing the people and lining their pockets.

Why does it seem like I have said this all before, why does it seem like we have all said this before? Why does it seem like the paycheck writers count on us becoming aware, questioning and developing a new sense of wanting to know just what the hell is going on when a law says it's for one thing, but it's really for another? Why do we always seem like we have to fight the same fight over and over again without really going anywhere?

Sometimes we go a little bit forward sometimes we go backwards before we progress forward. How do we build up energy so we can keep moving, and overcome adversity that is placed on us? But its more than adversity placed on us or that we place ourselves, it's that problems might not even be there in the first place if we didn't put faith in them.

All these distractions, these moral arguments, (whether some religions are better than others, what guns we can shoot and where, and whether everybody is equal to everybody else in every way or not) only exist because we buy into them.

I'm not saying those things don't happen because they do, what I'm saying is that they only have their power because we allow it. Basically it comes down to the old saying that we can't always change everything that goes on, but we can change how we respond to it.

We can go in knowing that there will always be people and events that try to shake us from our ingrained want for positive social change; and their power will get stronger the more they "think" they will succeed. We just have to stay focused, open, and remember why we started this journey in the first place.

ACTION MANIFESTO OF A MADMAN FOR GOOD

ENTRY#223

What motivates us to achieve bigger and better things? What gets us to turn the page and do everything differently than how we've done them before? How do we convince other people that even though they feel they can't move forward, they really can, they just might need to work a little harder and longer than the next guy?

Motivation can be a funny thing. It can be something that we think of, it can be something somebody else suggests, or it can be something that we observe. It can be something as simple as taking a walk out in the sun and seeing that there can be light among the darkness. It could be a friend or family member telling us we should get off our ass and do something because our dreams aren't going to fall into our laps, we might have to work for them.

Whatever form motivation takes, we can be assured that although it will be experienced differently, it's the same at its root for everybody. Motivation is something that drives us, something that connects us to something bigger and better than ourselves.

We can be sure that whatever our motivation is, we must be open to receive it. We could have all the motivation in the world right in front of us, (and the way forward could be obvious and almost easy looking) but if we aren't open or willing to accept what's being shown, we'll miss the path we're supposed to take because we weren't open to the motivation presented to us.

We must be open and honest about what we want out of life, nobody is going to do it for us. Motivation lies in the heart and head of an open minded person. Are we going to be open to it when the opportunity presents itself? Or are we going to just ignore it, not really want to do anything, not really care, but just go forward anyway?

Are we going to let motivation push us forward whether it comes from us or an outside influence? Or are we going to move forward blindly, trying to make our goals and dreams happen regardless of how we feel or if we're even motivated?

If we pay attention to what makes us tick, and what drives us forward, not only will we achieve our goals, but we will be motivated to achieve greater things because we allowed ourselves to.

ACTION MANIFESTO OF A MADMAN FOR GOOD

ENTRY#224

Once we start motivating ourselves (because we know what makes us happy and what drives us forward), we can put ourselves more in those environments and the real work can begin. How can we achieve positive social and political change if we aren't motivated to do the hard work required, or even know why we're doing it in the first place?

Motivation can be hard for somebody that has never consciously tried to be open to motivating factors, but the great thing is these factors are the same for everybody. Chances are a lot of us that aren't motivated or feel we can't be motivated really can be, we just aren't open to it. We must realize how we can be open, even though we can't tell in advance exactly what will drive us, because it's different for everybody.

What I can say is that we have to pay attention, we must be mindful. Like the old saying goes, "we never want to turn our back on our kids or the ocean", the same goes with motivation. It's not always about trying to gauge and guide and force through what solution we think is right; cause more often than not if we try to force it, everything will come out opposite of what we were thinking.

It's really about trusting the process and letting it work. We don't know how it will happen, where, when or even what form it will take when it happens. We just know that it will happen. I guess this might be a form of motivation in and of itself. Well, it can definitely be a starting off point; somewhere we can jump off of if we can't find a diving board.

Some might call it faith in the unknown or the unseen, this is true. But I call it taking an active and conscious role in our collective evolution. When we change ourselves, we change everybody around us. When we do that, we change the world.

ACTION MANIFESTO OF A MADMAN FOR GOOD

ENTRY#225

Why would somebody want to join a union, what is its purpose? Why is something like a union set up in the first place? Do workers really need protection?

A person might join a union so they have protection against the possible greed of the business owner or manager that sets employee wages so as to maximize profitability.

What would the wages of employees and workers be if there were no unions or organizations to protect their plight? Would the owners and managers be good and honest people that see somebody needs more than minimum wage to survive? Would they pay the workers as little money as possible, or just enough so the union won't call for a strike?

This is always an interesting dilemma. By joining a union you have money taken out of your paycheck, but you reap all the benefits that people have fought long and hard to get established. Some might say that we are just putting ourselves under the yoke of an overbearing organization that is just looking to control our every move.

Well, isn't that exactly what the business is trying to do, to control our every move by putting us in such a low paying position, and because we have many responsibilities (including family or simply just surviving), we don't rock the boat for fear of losing what few crumbs we have been thrown.

So, do we want control of our wages by having backup that will fight for us and not take any shit from our employer?

The question of whether or not to join a union might come down to figuring out who we think controls a person more, which is figured out by looking at the actual facts, not drowning ourselves in platitudes.

ACTION MANIFESTO OF A MADMAN FOR GOOD

ENTRY#226

Do we look for answers to the bigger problems in society by listening to a talking head, business owner, or other entity with an ulterior or profit motive behind what they're speaking about? Can we trust anything they're saying?

When people speak with a profit motive first, it changes the whole ball game. It can create a system where as much money is cranked out as possible, while managing commodities such as materials, utilities and workers are seen just as a numbers game. Whatever gets us bigger numbers is what we go for, no matter who it hurts.

This is the purpose of joining a union, so we have somebody behind us that doesn't have a profit motive first, but a "protect the worker" motive first. If we were an employee, who would we rather have backing us?

It basically comes down to do we want to go the fight alone, or do we want help? Do we want to go along blindly just happy to collect a paycheck, happy we aren't as bad off as the next guy? Or do we want something more?

ACTION MANIFESTO OF A MADMAN FOR GOOD

ENTRY#227

Do we want something more than the current situation we are in? Do we want to be stuck in the same old rut with the same old paycheck, the same old work environment and the same boss that doesn't know anything about anything?

We can change this dilemma. We can fix the problems that are plaguing the workplace. We can fight for a fair wage or maybe even some benefits that don't zap half our paycheck just for accepting them.

There have been many people in our history that have gone through different periods of depression. Whether it is an emotional and personal depression or an economic depression, it covers pretty much the whole system; which would probably make people depressed anyway, because they don't have a job, money or respect.

We have gone through depressions in many different forms since we started walking upright as humans, sometimes it all seems like part of the same cycle. The way we break that cycle is by standing up and saying "enough is enough; we aren't going to stand by and let you take advantage of us anymore."

ACTION MANIFESTO OF A MADMAN FOR GOOD

ENTRY#228

If we just stand by and let the steamroller of business and profit run us over, what kind of society would we have? Would it be a place where some of us are complete robots so stuck in survival mode that we would never rock the boat or risk not being accepted into the larger group because we didn't toe the line? Would we act like a mindless drone emptying our productivity into a hopper and only getting out a few coins?

There is no way a business can work without making a profit. There wouldn't be enough money to keep the lights on, buy materials, get permits, make repairs, or anything else that can come up on a complete random but somehow expected basis. That being said, the fastest way to increase profits, is to increase productivity.

When workers are productive, the business runs smooth, utilities and suppliers can be paid, and the business owners make profit. So the question comes up, how do we make sure the workers are productive? How do we make the sure the producers keep producing without walking off the job?

Maybe we are looking at profit all wrong, maybe we should be asking how we can keep the worker happy. How can we make the worker feel like a valued member of the team, I'm not talking about a laboratory created idea of being a valued team member, I'm talking about actual personal pride?

Once we start talking about paying workers a fair wage, giving them health benefits, an eight hour workday, weekends off and sick pay, then we might be getting somewhere. Maybe what we've been looking for has been right here under our nose the whole time.

Maybe the key is to look within ourselves and ask, what do we want, what do we deserve and what do we have a right to?

ACTION MANIFESTO OF A MADMAN FOR GOOD

ENTRY#229

We have a right to avoid being taken advantage of. We have the right to put in a productive day of work, then come home (which hopefully we have a home to come home to) and put our feet up with the satisfaction of knowing that our day had a purpose.

We also have the right to a fair living wage that allows us to not necessarily be rich, but just not to struggle and feel like every battle is an uphill battle. The more days we work and are complicit with the bad situation we might be in, we fall deeper and deeper into a hole of despair and debt.

We have the right to a work environment where we don't feel forced to accept a coworkers or boss's behavior for fear that we might be fired and made homeless. We have the right to be paid a fair wage that if god forbid we do get fired by some stupid boss for some stupid reason, we won't be made homeless; we will have had some money left over from our paycheck after paying bills that we were able to save.

We have the right to health benefits, so if we get sick or hurt we can go to the doctor and get healed or fixed. We have the right to be given a chance and not to be prejudged by how we look or what we might believe in. If we are to be judged on anything in the workplace at all, it should be on the quality of work that we produce.

We also have the right to be recognized for our achievements, to be congratulated when we've done well, and reprimanded when we have done badly; as long as in both cases there is a fair decision.

We have the right to a job and to be at least given the chance to be a productive member of society or the workforce. We have the power, we just have to join together with other people that do to. That is how we make change.

ACTION MANIFESTO OF A MADMAN FOR GOOD

ENTRY#230

We as workers must have our rights protected, because if we don't ensure them, who will? Who is the backbone of the workforce, the paycheck earners or the paycheck writers? Who is more important to a business, the person that punches a clock at 7am to put in an honest day of being productive, or the boss or secret partners that keep the lights on, provide the materials and space and offer guidance on how things should run?

The ongoing battle of who is more important to a business (the worker or the boss) has been going on for hundreds of years, and probably will go on way after this book is published. The point is to see and achieve the balance of all sides being of equal importance, and how everybody is an equal part of the whole package. Similar to the spokes on a wheel, if one spoke breaks or falls off, the wheel won't turn right, and has a good chance of running the whole car off the road.

Unions are in existence to level the playing field, to make sure workers are getting fair pay for the work they put in, and to ensure jobs are always existent by having happy employees that are cared for.

This will in turn make the business run better and also make it more profitable because the product or service that is turned out will be top notch. This will make the bosses happy because they will be successful and feel useful and worthwhile too, just like the worker.

ACTION MANIFESTO OF A MADMAN FOR GOOD

ENTRY#231

How much is it worth to have unions support us when we need help, and motivate us to work hard, ensuring balance is achieved between happiness, productivity and profit? Is it worth having a small amount taken out of our paycheck every month to give us the peace of mind that we can't be mindlessly fired for any reason, even if it's as stupid as the boss waking up on the wrong side of the bed?

How much is the idea of having someone in our corner worth? Is it worth a small percentage of our check to know that our pay at the end of the day will always be fair and honest for the work we put in?

We have the right to know what's going on. I know I have said "we have rights" a lot lately, because it's important to remember we do have rights. That we do have a voice and that we do matter.

By way of union dues, we can ensure that a voice is always fighting with the workers first on their mind. Balance can only be achieved when everyone involved is on the same playing field.

ACTION MANIFESTO OF A MADMAN FOR GOOD

ENTRY#232

Do we really want a level playing field, where all the players involved are playing by the same rules? Or do we want a game that always ends up in a lopsided victory with the victors crushing the losers just a little more each time?

Some people might even ask if a level playing field is even possible. Well, the game will never be fair if we keep saying it will never be fair. It's basically a self-fulfilling prophecy, if we will it strong enough and we think it so often that it works into our subconscious, it will change how we think.

If we want balance between the workers and the paycheck writers, we must realize that we're all in this together. By helping out one another, we help out each other. We can make all the changes we seek, (and we can make things fairer for all of us) but only if we are looking forward and side to side, and not just behind us.

ACTION MANIFESTO OF A MADMAN FOR GOOD

ENTRY#233

If we're looking side to side and then forward, is it possible that the balance of looking out for our own best interest and realizing we are all in this together the fuel that will propel us forward?

We get stuck in a lot of gunk in our society, there is a thick mud of political party, reputation, personal self-worth, the want to be better than the other guy, and a "just so some other guy will think we're cool" attitude that pervades everything. Is it because of capitalism, socialism, communism, terrorism, religion, just pure vanity, or is it something else?

Maybe the reason we get stuck and seem like we can't move or get anything done, (whether it be at home, work, the courts, or in congress) is that we can't see past what's right in front of us. I'm not saying that some people can't see past all the fog in front of them, because they can. All I'm saying is that we have an innate ability sometimes to doubt ourselves and our abilities.

Sometimes we need help being motivated to achieve the things we know we can achieve; sometimes we just need an extra push.

Humanism and accountability are ways to achieve balance and how we can fix most of the problems we get plagued with; this can be how we level the playing field and let everyone know that we are all human and striving to achieve the same basic goals.

ACTION MANIFESTO OF A MADMAN FOR GOOD

ENTRY#234

If humanism and accountability is how we achieve balance, (and that balance is what is going to level the playing field) will we automatically start moving towards our positive human evolution, and realize everyone is an equal member of the human team, or will we still have hiccups? Will we still get jealous of what the other person has? Will we still want to "one up" them cause it's what we have always done and it's so easy to do, and say "fuck all this new stupid stuff, I am better than that other guy and I deserve more than him, he is stupid."

Jealousy and negativity might still come up from time to time, actually it's almost a guarantee they will because they're human emotions. There is a balance of negative and positive, yin and yang whatever you want to call it, that keeps everything inline. If there wasn't the negative, we wouldn't know what the positive was. Also, if we didn't have the positive, we wouldn't know what the negative was. The polarities in life show us all the possibilities.

So when we're moving forward with our newfound positivity, we must remember, that whatever side we put more energy into will become more apparent to us. The other side will never completely go away, but the more significant side will be so because more energy got put into it in the first place.

ACTION MANIFESTO OF A MADMAN FOR GOOD

ENTRY#235

Achieving balance can be difficult, but is very well worth the effort put in. When we look around and see all of us are trying to achieve the same thing (just from different paths and trails), we begin to understand why we sometimes get caught up on little stuff.

The battles and arguments that we've had for a long time in this country and throughout the world have been about who amongst us is valued more, who deserves to be more well taken cared for, and who deserves more benefits because their work is deemed more important. All the reasons for war and heartache will continue until we slow down, stop and think.

The worker isn't more important than the employer, and the employer isn't more important than the worker, because if one didn't exist, neither would the other. It is a symbiotic relationship that will always work better when each side sees themselves as being treated fairly. And both sides are treated fairly when each side feels like they are actually being listened to, and not just being blown off.

Now that being said, since the battles that we're now in have been raging for a very long time, the sides are not starting at even and we can't all move forward in peace and harmony, yet; there has to be a lot of things righted before that happens. Taxes should be made fairer. When a CEO makes 400 times what their worker makes, there is no way they could see eye to eye and actually understand what the other is going through.

We must see each other through the others eyes, when we do, we get clarity. When we get clarity, we are on our first step towards balance. Once we have achieved balance, then we can walk together and move forward with peace and harmony towards our positive collective human evolution. But, balance can only be achieved when we take a look at the truth of what's around us, and actually and truly walk a mile in the other person's shoes.

ACTION MANIFESTO OF A MADMAN FOR GOOD

ENTRY#236

Does being a member of a union benefit the worker or the employer more? Would the average person gain more in benefits, pay, and vacation time, and become much more productive on the factory floor because they felt like they were taken care of if they weren't a union member? Would the boss benefit more with a union member workforce by having more productive employees? Would they lead the market by having the best quality products or services? Would bosses have respect amongst the community if the customer saw that the average worker was productive, taken care of, and also making more money? Or would it be balanced with each side benefiting equally, because they saw the other as actual people not a number? Would they know that they make the whole thing run because they're all in it together?

Thoughts can definitely swing back and forth about whether somebody believes they or anybody else should be a part of a union. The reasons can seem diametrically opposed if you only look at the surface. When you dig a little deeper, you will see that each side plays an equal part, just like a spoke on a wheel or a car motor where everything has to be working in unison for it to turn over and stay running.

The point is that all we really need to work together is for us to see that we aren't on opposing sides, we're just on different parts of the same side.

ACTION MANIFESTO OF A MADMAN FOR GOOD

ENTRY#237

Being a member of a union, a boss or a manager is like being on the same coin, just different sides. Some people might say that when you're a member of a union it's like heads you win tails you lose for the manager. The unions "as they say" will zap all their money and power by way of paying the workers way too much, causing them to not have anything left to grow with, therefore they would just shrivel and die.

Some people might say that when we're a boss who has union employees it is "heads you win tails you lose" for the workers because they remember how unions of the past struggled and fought for everything, (the 8 hour work day, weekends off and sick time etc...). If unions have been decimated since the eighties and aren't nearly as powerful as they used to be, the workers will fight the boss, think they have the powerful backing like workers years before, and when that help doesn't come, the boss will steam roll over them and take everything they have. The lesser the pay and benefits the workers get, the more money the bosses can stuff in their pockets.

A lot of people talk and a lot of people say a lot of things. The difference is that all of us are all part of the same argument, whether we are against unions because we think they benefit the workers or the manager more, or are for unions for the same reason. We must realize unions benefit people equally even if we can't see the other side as just being another side.

ACTION MANIFESTO OF A MADMAN FOR GOOD

ENTRY#238

When we talk about the pay that unions have earned for their members, we should also talk about what pay scales would be like if unions weren't around. If managers had no guidelines for paying their employees and could pay them whatever they wanted, do we think they would give better pay on their own accord? Do we think out of the goodness of their heart bosses would go up to workers and say, "hey, you don't need to work on the weekends. I know you have a life and work so hard during the week, you deserve some time off to rest and to spend time with your family."

What about giving workers sick time? Would bosses have gone up to a sick employee and said they could go home and take the next couple days off with pay, (and without the fear of getting fired) if it weren't for unions? Would they have offered pregnancy leave, overtime pay, minimum age requirements for workers or a minimum wage (that doesn't really keep up with inflation anyways) as a baseline that they can't pay below?

I guess the point is would companies have done all this stuff with their employees not being member of unions? Would the person at the top of the food chain have given more to the person on the bottom of the food chain if they weren't forced to by a collective group with one voice, fighting for the same things for all of the masses?

Whether we believe bosses would do things on their own accord or let the market dictate, (or whether we believe coalesced people with one goal and one aim putting their voices together to gain strength are the way things really are) both ideas ring true. We believe what we see when we don't actually do anything by ourselves.

ACTION MANIFESTO OF A MADMAN FOR GOOD

ENTRY#239

So they're these two opposing sides, one that believes being a member of a union will benefit all of society by providing for the workers. Or the other side that says being a member of a union will benefit none of society; the bosses will go out of business when they have to raise prices so high because of the union's demands, and will have to fire and lay off people because of it.

We know all this; the difference is what do we do with this knowledge? Do we take it and make the unions stronger, or we do we take the information and tear them down? Which way will we go?

I think the answer lies in how we look at the world. Do we believe in fighting, striving, achieving and moving forward with making only our lives better and the people closest to us, because everyone else is seen as an obstacle? Or do we see that everybody and everything is interconnected, and care about making everybody's lives better because we see how everything affects everything else?

ACTION MANIFESTO OF A MADMAN FOR GOOD

ENTRY#240

Whether we care about other people than ourselves, might dictate whether we would join and be a member of a union or not. If we only care about ourselves, would we still join a union? Would we see how the union can benefit us personally, how with their help we can ensure we will be treated fairly and have somebody standing up and speaking out for us when the voice coming from above is much louder and much more powerful than ours?

There are some of us out there that see the benefits of unions, what they've earned for the workers and how they've stood up for them and say hey, "this can really benefit me and build me up and make me better than the guy next to me that isn't part of the union."

By inadvertently joining and being a member of a union for our sole benefit, we are benefiting the whole because we are a community of workers; and even if somebody isn't a member, they still benefit because bosses have to pay attention to the market. Members of that same union make standing up for collective rights possible.

With this new revelation, we might hear that by benefiting ourselves we are benefiting the whole, that individualism, self-preservation and getting the most gold for ourselves is the best thing anybody could possibly do.

But, what we don't seem to realize or maybe we don't care to, is that we can be an individual within a group setting that benefits us, and everybody else at the same time.

ACTION MANIFESTO OF A MADMAN FOR GOOD

ENTRY#241

Is tricking somebody into doing the right thing, ever the right thing to do? Do we have to authentically know about what every inch of something looks and feels like for us to believe in it or go after it? Would we be able to go after something we thought sounded good and benefited us and only us, but really benefited the whole group; and when we found out about it, would we be able to handle it, would it blow our mind?

Sometimes we don't know what is best for us. Of course what's hard to swallow is the same people that proclaim what's best for us, are still people, so how would they know what is best for anybody?

We go through life and do the best we can. If we can benefit the world and make humanity a little bit brighter, (even for a short time) we should take the chance because memories last forever.

If we know that somebody is working towards something they think is one way, and we think is another, we shouldn't trick them into anything. If they are a benefit to themselves, they are benefiting society by not being a detriment. For them to really feel, hold and carry out the right thing, they have to want to.

We as a people must realize that we all arrive from different paths, but are going after many of the same goals. Sometimes the way we get there is very unconventional and something like we've never seen before. If we are open, we see its true importance.

ACTION MANIFESTO OF A MADMAN FOR GOOD

ENTRY#242

This understanding of different paths (and how we're all going after the same basic things just from different "paths") helps us to be open, to have a starting point to work from in our enlightenment.

Maybe all we have to do to truly understand what we're looking for and what we're going after is just to stop, slow down and look. I know I have touched on this topic many times throughout my manifesto series, but it is the root of many of the things that help make up the bigger picture.

Basically, we just have to stop and smell the roses; see what's around, see the beauty that exists everywhere (that we might ignore) as we plow through our mind numbing routines thinking, nothing will ever change.

If somebody is a member of a union, they're taking the path they think is right for themselves, their families, and the environment around them whether they consciously think about it or not. We might think that a union member is out to destroy all the great democratic institutions this country has built up over the years by being a member of a communist group; that they want to dictate to the paycheck writers how much money they should earn and everything the boss should do.

If one of us thinks this, we should slow down and look at the reality that's in front of us, (not use what's in front of us to mean something that uses false definitions to describe itself). Actually <u>SEEING</u> what's in front of us is the key.

ACTION MANIFESTO OF A MADMAN FOR GOOD

ENTRY#243

Seeing what's in front of us can be the key to unlock our misunderstanding, if we realize that most of what causes our misunderstanding is ourselves. Sometimes when we don't comprehend something or we don't like something, it's because of a perceived notion that we either learned or gained by listening to some false prophet on the magic idiot box. Or we might have heard it in a book, movie magazine or whatever caught our eye by advertising with sometimes flashy colors and beautiful people who we wish we were.

This is where stopping and slowing down to see what's in front of us can be a good thing. If we just stop and think for a moment, we would see what the other side is trying to pull by playing on our insecurities and fears; making us believe that if we conform to how they think a person should look and act, we will fulfill the commodity role they see us as. All this will cause the whole machine to run until the end of time because nobody sees that what it will take to stop it is enough people to stop and think, and go hey, wait a minute…….

ACTION MANIFESTO OF A MADMAN FOR GOOD

ENTRY#244

Unions are most effective when all their members actively see and knowingly act on what's in front of them. If a union's membership all were members because they wanted to be, and saw the use of having a large group of people at their back, they would know that without a large voice, the paycheck writers would probably not do a whole lot for the betterment of the worker (unless it was at a snail's pace).

If some union members weren't members because they wanted to be, but because they had to be (or they couldn't have their job), it benefits them anyway. If workers aren't part of a union even though other workers in their same trade are, they would still benefit. Just the fact that there is a union, would raise the industry standards and force non-union employers to comply, or be rendered un-effective in the market place (because they were going against their own orthodoxy and not letting the market dictate).

We band together sometimes and attempt to right the wrongs of the whole group. Sometimes we only work to better ourselves. Life is more conscious and seems to work better for all of us when everybody is honest with themselves in where they stand, and where they're going.

ACTION MANIFESTO OF A MADMAN FOR GOOD

ENTRY#245

When there is no way to be a member of a union because one doesn't exist, what do we do then? Are standards going to automatically lower in our community because there is no large group fighting for us? Are we going to be better off because nobody is dictating to the paycheck writers what they should or shouldn't do, causing them to do whatever makes them the most money?

Knowing if a union in our area will fix the problem as we see it now is hard to say. What I can say for sure is if we band together, and actually work from the same place that we know about anyway, we will get where we want to go more often than not.

What do we have to lose if not for a little bit of our time? Try it, go out into the world, find a problem that needs fixing, find others that feel the same way, (help those of us that don't), try putting your voice together with others and see what can be done. When voices come together over an alleged injustice, and speak unified towards a goal or future that hits at the heart of humanity because it's the basic essence of what we're all looking for, we should listen. When we are a member of a union, there is something special going on, something that tells us that we are taking an active role in our own betterment. What do you think??

ACTION MANIFESTO OF A MADMAN FOR GOOD

ENTRY#246

If a company or businesses' bottom line is making as much money as it can for itself and its shareholders, is a union a complete antithesis to what they're stated goals are? If a union is allowed to flourish, (or it does so even if it's not allowed because the bosses can't do anything when the workers stand up) will the business fail because they will have to give the people a little extra? Would they not grow as fast as they would otherwise if they were paying the people the least amount they could, just short of having workers starving on the floor? What battles will show up when all this is being decided?

They are many things that need to be sorted out when a union is finding its footing among the workplace or place of business, especially if the paycheck writers are hostile to their very presence; they might even disagree sometimes, in fact they will disagree a lot.

If unions and companies remember what they're really fighting for, what the effects of those actions will be and how they are really created, they will see that they agree way more of the time then when they disagree.

A happy employee is a productive employee. A productive employee is someone that makes the business run smoother because the product or service they turn out is of much higher quality because it was created out of want, not out of fear.

Workers that are happy work better, isn't that what a business wants?

ACTION MANIFESTO OF A MADMAN FOR GOOD

ENTRY#247

How do we make a happy worker? How do we make a worker feel that he or she is taken care of; make them feel they're treated like a real person in the way they're talked to and the way they're paid? How do we create a business at the top of an industry and at the top of workers lists of places they definitely want to apply to? How do we make a place appealing to the business world and to the workers world? Would this balance make business more valuable on Wall Street because people see soaring profit and an unmatched productivity when workers churning out the products and services feel they are worthwhile members of the team? Both sides of this fight, the boss that wants their business to run well and be successful and profitable, and the worker who wants to make a decent living with benefits, (the parties who want to be talked to and treated like a human being), basically are fighting for the same thing.

Oh it may look like fighting when the bosses say the workers want too much money, and because of the heavy handed union asking for too high a benefits for their members, it's causing the company to go out of business.

The workers say they want what is fair, they just want to live out what the stereotypical American dream is, own a house have a family, put the kids through college, have a retirement.

Aren't they just fighting from two sides of the same coin?

ACTION MANIFESTO OF A MADMAN FOR GOOD

ENTRY#248

If a coin has two sides, and a battle has two sides, (at least the two sides that are the most apparent because they're the ones with the loudest voices) aren't they still part of the same unit? Aren't they fighting for two parts of the same thing? Aren't they really fighting for the same thing when it comes down to it, but aren't able to see it because they are both blinded by not only preconceived notions but also fervor and rage?

Let's just take the fight for a minimum wage. The workers want fair pay to live on because the wages that were around before minimums were instituted wasn't nearly enough, and was at the whim of the paycheck writer who could change it as often as the wind blows. The boss might see arguing for a living wage as some of us rising up and trying to tell them what to do, and trying to bring down the business by not making it profitable.

Well that might be the question to ask, is the place of work still profitable? Are customers still coming in when the workers are paid below a minimum standard of pay, and under a minimum level of safety standards that would not only keep them safe, but also the customer that decides to buy?

Workers might always have to fight for what they believe is a fair rate of pay and benefits, but the battle will be won when the people they're battling, see that they are only making the business stronger.

ACTION MANIFESTO OF A MADMAN FOR GOOD

ENTRY#249

How does a business become stronger and more profitable, how do they're paycheck writers make more money amidst the windfall they might already be stuffing in their pocket? Do they take the route of companies like Wal-Mart, and move to control every stage of the supply chain, and have a say from the field all the way through production at the factories and where and how it shows up at our stores?

Do they just farm everything out and really have no factories or no store front, and have all other entities run every other part of the business from everything to the mailroom, the shipping, the making, the driving?; basically every part of the business is farmed out and they don't control the supply chain, they guide the supply chain by making sure the people running it are doing what they are supposed to do. Or does a business make what they can by being the best with safety, regulations, employee satisfaction and loyalty by paying workers not extravagant amounts, but what they are actually worth because it is actual pay that allows them to make an actual living which actually allows them to not struggle?

Which way a business goes can tell you a lot about the person or board of directors that run it and what consciousness level they're at.

The big idea is that business runs smoother when an employee doesn't have to fight hard every day for a bigger paycheck, and when a paycheck writer doesn't always have to fight with the worker over the amount of that paycheck.

ACTION MANIFESTO OF A MADMAN FOR GOOD

ENTRY#250

Does a business run smoother when the pay check writers and the paycheck earners aren't fighting all the time? Is an outlet more profitable when the union isn't marching at the front door with thousands of people yelling, singing and demanding at any and all people that try to go in the front door, discouraging them so they go to the next union store down the street? Is a place more profitable when it pays its workers whatever it wants?

Many battles have occurred through history over everything from the right to organize, to arguing for better conditions, to many of the things the average protester may take for granted. Days of strike breakers seems so distant, almost like a story grandpa used to tell about what happened when he was a young troublemaker.

These battles happened because people wanted a basic standard of living, and wanted to feel a little less like indentured servants or like the share croppers of the twenties who could never quite get out of debt (not to mention have to have their 6 year olds work in the coal mine). How could these people hope to have a normal life with an education that might actually get them somewhere?

We have to avoid these battles when we can by looking at the root problems. We must ask why things are actually happening, not what are both sides saying are actually happening.

Sometimes both sides are just looking to dupe people over to their way of thinking.

When we slow down and think about not only what is happening right in front of us, but also what actually works for both sides, (because we know that one side can't run without the other) we will see that we are a lot closer to agreeing than the media makes it seem.

ACTION MANIFESTO OF A MADMAN FOR GOOD

ENTRY#251

To get past endless cycles of battles, or better put, to get to a point collectively as a society where battles don't need to be fought anymore, we need to look at the root of why they happen in the first place.

Why are businesses really arguing that a raise of the minimum wage will destroy their business, is it because they will have to raise prices far beyond what the average one of us is willing or able to pay? Why are unions arguing that raising the minimum wage will benefit the business because not only will the workers be more productive, but the money that gets fed back into the economy is ten-fold than what is put in the first place?

Protesting workers and union strikers used to get in some bloody battles with employer paid strike breaking thugs; they only ended when a bunch of people were hurt, some killed, but many went to the hospital. These historic scenes of battling between paycheck writer and paycheck earner would put the Wisconsin and Ohio battles to shame. Not to take anything away from the two states, they stood up for what they believed in, and that should never be talked bad about. But they didn't have to fight back against full on violence from the paycheck writers. We must remember that it doesn't have to come to that.

If both sides would just listen to each other, (especially with the boss side listening to the workers side because a lot of room needs to be made up till it's an even playing field) we would all be better off.

If the boss listened to the worker and realized the union is there to help with business, than the unions would listen to the business leaders more, and everything would run a lot smoother. It's amazing to see what can be gained by hearing not just listening to the other side.

ACTION MANIFESTO OF A MADMAN FOR GOOD

ENTRY#252

Compromise can be a powerful thing when trying to avoid a battle, but at the same time, battles must not be avoided when they are the only option after every other possible way of doing things has been exhausted.

First of all, compromise is not a dirty word. Some of us lately have tossed around the idea that compromise isn't an option, and we must never shy away from our ideas, how we feel inside ourselves, and the way we would like and deserve to be treated. At the same time, we have to stick to our ideas so we can be an equal part in that compromise, and not just be steamrolled by the other sides ideas. It has to be a balance.

Standing up for what we believe in is always the right way to go, that's why being on one side is helpful in trying to negotiate a compromise in the first place. The question comes up sometimes, when do we compromise and when do we fight ahead? When do we realize that we can win if only we fight hard enough, because some of the hardest fought battles were won because people stuck them out? And when do we realize that the other side has us and we retreat or compromise? Or maybe we agree so as to avoid further violence?

Whatever the reason for a compromise, whenever it should come up for whatever reason, we have to remember that sometimes it needs to be done, and we should never ridicule the idea so much that it isn't even a possibility.

ACTION MANIFESTO OF A MADMAN FOR GOOD

ENTRY#253

If compromise is a viable option and not a dirty word, and fighting is a viable option when compromise is not possible, (or we feel so strongly for our side that we feel there is no other option but to fight) when or if, will the battle begin? When do things reach a boiling point, what are the variables that seem to set the situation aflame because passions are allowed to get a little too heated?

Battles can take many forms, whether they are actual physical fighting battles, verbal protests, beat back battles, speaking in front of congress, arguing in court, mental battles, or more of a war of ideas, an ideological war if you will.

The idea is that battles can happen at any time, and on the same token, compromise can happen at any time. If we are open, conscious and authentically paying attention to what's around us, then we will be able to tell if a battle is worth our time.

If we pay attention a little more too how we feel, how others feel and the consequences and goals that both sides have and are willing to endure for, then we will know what our purpose is.

There is no black and white answer to almost anything in the world. Somebody just can't tell us what to think and when to think it, the most they can do is to guide us in the right direction. The best thing we can do is pay attention to the signs around us, we never know what's coming around the bend; trust the process, let it work.

ACTION MANIFESTO OF MADMAN FOR GOOD

ENTRY#254

Figuring out there is no black and white answer to just about anything in life because we all take in information differently, could be akin to our the world being flipped around. It might be so different than we've ever thought before, that to realize society actually runs differently than we thought, would cause our heads to metaphorically explode and cause the world to completely change again.

Saying there is no easy answer to our real problems seems like it rolls off the tongue with no effort or much thought. What if I were to propose something different, what if the problems were that easy to solve? What if the answers to most of the problems we get plagued with could be fixed by ideas we already know about, but might have ignored or forgot about because of life's routines? What if solutions are right in front of us, just waiting for us to take advantage?

The problem is easy but it's hard at the same time. I realize hearing that sounds like somebody saying the sky is only blue because we think it's blue. The idea to remember is that the sky is above us all, and the sky will look a little different to everybody for a million different reasons.

What we should remember when we're thinking about workers' rights, and what bosses should do when they're hiring and employing workers, is that all of us are human. We are all looking for the same basic things. If we could just put ourselves in somebody else's shoes and actually walk around for a few days, we would feel what the other person feels; then and only then will we truly empathize with the other side in a battle for who we really are. Only when we see the other side as ourselves, will we actually be able to do something that benefits ourselves.

ACTION MANIFESTO OF A MADMAN FOR GOOD

ENTRY#255

Walking around in somebody else's shoes, feeling comfortable in our own skin, (whatever other metaphor we want to come up with) is apt when trying to figure out not only our own psyche, but also how to deal with the world.

Treating somebody how we would like to be treated doesn't only work for five year olds in kindergarten; it also works for adults in all walks of life, even if we are amidst an ideological battle for the good of humanity. If the paycheck writer actually knew and felt what the worker was going through and the sacrifices they had to make, (sometimes on what bill to pay and what bill could be put off) they might not be as hesitant when the worker is asking for a small raise in cost of living adjustments.

If the worker and paycheck earner was able to see their boss as a human being because the person treated them well and saw eye to with them, (and didn't feel threatened by them if they made the wrong move) then maybe when the boss had to cut hours or benefits, the worker would actually believe them because they would see how the person didn't really want to do it, they had to; and since they are seen as humans, than they are seen as having the human emotion of actually feeling bad for the other side.

Battles can be avoided if we see the other side as ourselves because we wouldn't want to fight, beat up or kill ourselves. Compromise can be achieved when both sides don't judge each other. Success can be achieved when everybody is lifted up and made to feel part of the process.

ACTION MANIFESTO OF A MADMAN FOR GOOD

ENTRY#256

Overcoming stereotypes can be a difficult task in our private lives, let alone when we're a member of an organization and get labeled by the side we're fighting against; of course whenever there is an opposing view to our own, there is really no telling how it will be described. An opposing side might try to put their opponent inside a nice pretty little wrapped box that is easy to open and easy to understand its contents.

The question may come up that since we know that stereotypes are out there, what if anything can we do to combat them? If somebody calls a union just a bunch of Nazi pinko communists that don't want to do an honest day's work for an honest day's pay, and always ask for more until it costs the paycheck writers so much money that they have to fire people, or close down and move to China, nothing will change.

The boss would probably love to move to China anyway because not only will their business run cheaper, but they get a tax break for business expenses for moving their factory; they end up paying nothing for it even though many Americans could lose their jobs, and be thrown out of their homes just so the owner can get that Chinese factory.

We must watch out for stereotypes because they can tear us down and destroy our lives; they can also show us that no matter what somebody says about us, usually, it turns out not to be true. Projection is apparent in much of our interactions involving people with different views.

ACTION MANIFESTO OF A MADMAN FOR GOOD

ENTRY#257

What is a stereotype; is it something somebody thinks is true about a person or a whole group of people not necessarily based on fact, but based on supposed experience? Of course this experience turns out to be not nearly as true as is believed. Unless this person has met every person on earth, and knows how all those people behave and react in every situation, then stereotypes can't possibility be true.

Unions and workers fighting for their rights have had to overcome countless stereotypes for years when they bump up against the paycheck writers that want to soak a little bit more from their skill and ability "bank" than the day before. They are used to how the other side acts, or at least they know how they react, which is by not paying attention and telling themselves that the other person doesn't know what they're talking about and shouldn't be taken seriously.

The question comes up, can people avoid these stereotypes completely? Can somebody step into the fray of ideological warfare and say without a doubt that they will be able to avoid stereotypes and unfair assumptions?

Maybe the question isn't about avoiding stereotypes, but simply learning how to not take them seriously; and remembering that they were created by somebody who is ignorant and doesn't know and doesn't want to know about how the other side works. If we do, we already have the other side beat.

ACTION MANIFESTO OF A MADMAN FOR GOOD

ENTRY#258

If we are in battle or an argument, or some other instance when we're trying to change someone's opinion and they start to generalize, should we generalize back so as to stoop to their level? Should we just stand above the fray and play the silent observer? Can we can listen and take everything in and give our opinion later? Should we comment, question and bring up every single thing that the other person says that we don't agree with? This may make us feel good, but will completely stifle the conversation and make it grind to a halt.

Workers have been called every name in the book. When we get a job, what do we usually want out of it? We want to be able to make a decent living, support our family and be able to put food on the table while paying bills. When we feel we're being unfairly treated and that our standard of living has gone down despite all the hard work we have put in, we must stand up and fight if we want to achieve our dreams. Sometimes, this act of standing up makes the opposing side (the paycheck writers) introduce many sides of the story, "oh we can't do it for this reason or we can't do it for that reason, but the reason is we can't do it"; when the whole time they really can.

When the workers find out that management can afford the modest cost of living adjustments they seek, should they resort to name calling and generalization by calling people at the top "the fats cats", the elitist out of touch people that have no idea what the average person is thinking because they have completely different needs and goals?

Does name calling drive passions to get more people to join the fight for a cause and drive them to achieve the things they only dream about? Does this put them on the same level playing field as the people who call them good for nothing commie pinkos that don't want to do an honest day's work?

Ask yourself, what would you respond better to?

ACTION MANIFESTO OF A MADMAN FOR GOOD

ENTRY#259

If achieving our goals includes leveling the playing field for everybody so we get treated like we should be treated (and are able to make a living that is actually a living), should we also level the playing field for the way we think as well? Should somebody stoop down to their opponent's level to understand what they're talking about? Do we have to resort to name calling and unfair generalizations to fully describe what the problem is? Or do we do this because we don't really know enough about what the other person thinks and wants to do? Is it just easier and quicker to just say the first thought that comes to mind and just go with it?

We must never lose ourselves when we're fighting for what we believe in or standing up for things we and everybody else deserves in the workplace and beyond. We must always remember who we are when we are trying to better society, because if we don't, and we forget who we are (and lose ourselves amidst the fog of the average back and forth), what have we really improved?

If we defeat the opposing side by basically acting the same as our opponents but from a different perspective, does that make us just as bad as them? When somebody wants to attack us (and they do), but they say their real aims aren't destroying our way of life and way of thinking, they will have done just that, if we are constantly looking over our shoulders.

Once we find ourselves, we must never lose ourselves. It's like when we see stuff that's swept under the rug, once we know it's under there, that's it. There is no unknowing it.

ACTION MANIFESTO OF A MADMAN FOR GOOD

ENTRY#260

Is learning new things in the world the right goal? The reason we wake up every morning and get out of our bed is to see what the new day will bring, right? If we always do what we have always done, how can we ever expect different results? If we expect to beat our opponent by becoming just as bad as them by using their methods and tactics, we have lost ourselves amidst the fight; and although they might have lost this particular battle, they have won the war because their goal of getting us to change to be more like them, worked.

When paycheck writers try to pay their workers less and use explanations that don't reach the people, (they might say the business doesn't have enough money, or the debt on their balance sheet doesn't add up to what the accountant wants it to be) does it actually speak to the actual worker? Do workers have an accountant or even a need for a balance sheet when they're just trying to make ends meet and decide which bill they can afford to pay, and which one to put off?

This is when management fails to get what they want; when the workers don't see eye to eye with them and just goes along with whatever they say. If the worker wants more from their place of employment and from their boss, all they have to do is let their boss talk. The boss thinks they're getting ahead by trying to explain and going into more detail, but in actuality it only cements cynicism because they're doing what they think the worker wants to hear instead of what they actually need to hear.

We and only we know what we truly need. Somebody else or some other outside entity can't put us into a little box and wrap it up in a pretty little package unless we let them, unless we just say hey, "whatever that person says must be true because they have more power than me." Well, if we slow down and look at what paycheck writers are really doing, we will find they actually have less power than us, and are very scared that we will figure that out.

ACTION MANIFESTO OF A MADMAN FOR GOOD

ENTRY#261

The question of who is farther ahead in an argument can be completely subjective. Just because somebody says they are big and powerful, doesn't necessarily mean they are. On the same token, if somebody says they're weak, powerless and can't do anything, it doesn't necessarily mean they are useless.

So, where do we stand when workers are fighting to get what they deserve from their paycheck writers, do they just not believe anything the other side says? What if (as there are exceptions to every rule) there happens to be one instance where an actual honest person that truly wants to work with their employees and make their lives better unlike many of their predecessors?

If we're blinded by what we think about the other side, and have a feeling that we're so sure what they're going to do that we don't pay attention to their actions, we might miss something really important. It's like when some people say we shouldn't pay attention to the media because it's all bullshit, funded by people that all have sinister agendas.

While some of this might be true, if we don't pay attention to everything that's going on in front of us, (instead of giving in to some preconceived notion of what we think is going on) we will miss the few kernels of truth that spill out which are present in all things. We just have to slow down and stop to see them.

Stereotypes are a way that both sides can be blinded to what's actually going on in front of them; the biggest thing we can do to overcome this, is pay attention to what we actually see, not what we think we see, mindfulness.

ACTION MANIFESTO OF A MADMAN FOR GOOD

ENTRY#262

The question comes up sometimes, how do we pay attention to what we see when there is so much information and so many events flying by our face on a daily basis that we can't possibly absorb them all? With things flying at us from all directions (not to mention all throughout our daily lives, jobs and whatever other routine we have), how do we absorb what's good and add it to the top of the pile? How can we pay attention to everything and still be able to do anything?

I think the question isn't so much how we can pay attention to all things that happen, (because that is not humanely possible without some kind of robot brain) I think the question or better yet, the best thing we can do is to just be open, and do the best we can. We must be mindful and pay attention to what's around us the best we can while we go through our daily interactions. We don't have to stop our routine, or even slow it up; in actuality we are enhancing our routine when we see what the real and true meaning of it is.

The more we pay attention, the more we will see. And the more that we see , the more we will figure out, and the more we figure out, the more problems we will be able to solve for ourselves and the people around us and beyond. It's not a fool proof idea, and it won't work every time, but what in life can be? We can't possibly absorb everything, but it's guaranteed the more we are open and pay attention, the better chance we will absorb what's actually important.

ACTION MANIFESTO OF A MADMAN FOR GOOD

ENTRY#263

It can be hard for some us to pay attention like we never have before. We might be one of those people that just cruised by in life, had a job, came home, tried to pay the bills, tried to have a life and a family and have some food and nice place to sleep. But, we might have never paid attention to what's happening around us, what it all means. We might not have ever given much thought to why we work hard and never seem to get ahead. Why the boss seems to just get richer and richer while our standard of living hasn't gone up at all.

If we have never thought this way, and our life hasn't turned out how we would have liked, why do we keep doing things the same way over and over and over while expecting different results? This either signifies genius because we are able to see past our current situation, or we are insane because we don't see what's right in front of us even though it's a big sign with bright flashing lights and a siren just for good measure.

Do we want to change things? Do we want a better situation for ourselves, our family, friends and everybody else on the planet? To change things we might have to try them a little differently, we might have to change our way of thinking and doing and actually see and think about what's in front of us.

We must not use stereotypes which can be the easy way out by allowing us not to think about what's in front of us, and lets us float by with some other more comfortable notion.

To make change, sometimes it can be uncomfortable; sometimes it can be scary, and sometimes it will flip the whole world upside down from what we're used to. The thing is though, if we want to achieve all the things we dream about, we have to go out and get them, we can't wait for them to fall into our laps.

ACTION MANIFESTO OF A MADMAN FOR GOOD

ENTRY#264

As people, a nation and a world community, we have many different thoughts, feelings and actions we feel we must or must not take that we feel very strongly about. There are many opinions about how things should be or how things should be more like they used to be.

There are many thoughts about how we should move forward. Should we travel with our blinders on and only see what's ahead of us, moving forward towards our goals without ever looking side to side? Do we move forward while taking everything into account with the opposite of blinders on, and keep our eyes and our ears completely wide open?

To overcome preconceived notions and stereotypes we must remember that we are individuals, that we are all different. On the same accord, we are all the same at the basic root of our soul of how we would like to be treated (our true feelings about humanity and the world, might only exist in our subconscious, and we might not want to admit it).

We have to be open and willing to hear what's out there. When we aren't, (and we just go forward without learning) we're always thinking people and the world are a certain way so there is no point in giving any thought to how situations could be different or how they could be changed; which is exactly where stereotypes and generalizations come from. When we don't know about something, and don't want to know, it's basically ignorance.

"Ignorance is the root of all evil."

ACTION MANIFESTO OF A MADMAN FOR GOOD

ENTRY#265

Do we all believe ignorance exists? Do all of us believe people are always open to what others think? Since there aren't any problems in the world, do we have to do anything different or can we go on as business as usual? Do we believe we're all just ignorant beasts, only looking out to destroy the person on the sides of us just so we can get a little bit ahead of them?

I think most of the world falls somewhere in the middle, the big sweet spot called the gray area where most of us live and continue to exist. There is no way to generalize about almost anything because to know for sure beyond a shadow of a doubt, we would have to meet every person in the world, go everywhere and be amongst everything in every situation (which is a feat that Santa Claus couldn't even could pull off).

So the next time somebody tries to tell us they know everything about a certain situation, know every type of person, or how all people of a certain group will always act, ask them a question. Are they the end all be all that has all the answers? Are they the one that has done everything and has met everybody? Cause if they haven't, they should just stop talking, go to the back of the line, and not come back up front until they are able to step forward with their eyes and their mind open.

ACTION MANIFESTO OF A MADMAN FOR GOOD

ENTRY#266

If we're looking ahead to see what we can accomplish, are we also looking to see what has held us back so we don't make the same mistakes twice? Are we blinding ourselves to what's happened before, trying to block it from our memory, so we can give ourselves the false idea of a clean slate? Should we take the time to feed our souls with the fuel we need to move forward? Should we avoid what drags us down because by going after what we don't really want overall but might want for the moment, (casting our net so wide that most of what we catch we don't want) it causes our chances of getting what we really want to be very slim? We need to seek out soul nurturing activities and reject soul killing activities.

We must never stop thinking about our future or moving forward. There are going to be times when we get lonely, upset or depressed causing us to think or do what we know is detrimental to our soul but do it anyway because it makes us happy for the moment; in in the end it will slow and eventually stop our progress.

We have to remember what's really important and what we really want. Then, have that thought permeate through our minds and our souls so there is no way in hell we could ever forget, because it is and always will be the first thing on our mind. If a time should come where we begin to lose our confidence, and leave ourselves open to every possibility in the world because peace of mind for the moment is the only thing that matters, we should slow down, stop and think.

What is this moment really doing for our outlook? Is this action something that we would normally do? Is it something that we have never thought about the consequences of and what can happen to our way of thinking if we continue going this way?

If we continue down a path we know is not good for us, but we go down it anyway, we are in trouble of losing who we are. We will lose our souls and nothing in life will feel worth doing because we feel we have no control over our thoughts and actions. But that's the thing, we do. We do have control of our actions and our thoughts. We can end those actions that are detrimental to us at any time once we realize that we're good enough and worth it enough to have something better; something that makes us be better people and better stewards of the planet.

Sometimes we need help in moving forward, sometimes we need a little push so we not only start off in the right direction, but also so we keep moving in the right direction when we get perplexed. Sometimes we find ourselves at a crossroads where we must decide which way to go because the possibilities are there for us to either achieve greatness, or be just another statistic; we could be somebody who blew their talents because we couldn't focus our mind in the right direction, even though the material we write about is the main subject of its contents.

We can do better, we can do what is best for us, and we can make ourselves smile. We have the ability to make our soul shine, but sometimes we have to remember to flip the switch that turns the light on in the first place. Sometimes we have to plug into the right outlet that will provide light, and not darkness. We own the keys to our soul and our way of moving forward; we just have to pick them up and get our energy focused in a way that it's not being used on stuff we don't give a shit about.

If we waste our energy on something we don't care about, there will be nothing left to spend on what we do care about. And what would we rather spend our energy on, something we know will continuously make us unhappy but do it anyway, or something that builds us up, makes our soul sing, and makes us want to move forward because we feel the loving and warm energy pulling us in the right direction. How do we want to expend our energy?

Basically it boils down to, do we want our energy to be wasted on something we don't want anyway? Or do we want our energy to be spent on something that will replenish what's expended because the action it produces is what makes our soul sing, and fills up our cup.

We have the ability to empty our cup, smash it to smithereens and to make sure it never holds anything again. But, we also have the ability to not only fill it up, but also to have actions and thoughts that will continuously replenish it so we always have some left for ourselves, for our well-being, and that of the world. That way, when we go to save the world, we actually can and not just talk about it.

Now is the time for positive action, we are ready. We just have to continuously remind ourselves of the fact ☺

ACTION MANIFESTO OF A MADMAN FOR GOOD

ENTRY#267

So how do we avoid the probable collapse of any kind of workable relationship between the paycheck writers and the pay check earners? Is there a way we can compromise so as to avoid making both of our lives worse by shutting down the whole system and putting both sides out of work? What kind of people will it take to prove to the world that workers are the grease that makes the wheels turn, and if they won't get paid a fair wage with livable benefits, (so they can actually go the doctor when they get sick) they will walk off the job. The old workers will make it clear to any prospective employees, they better plan on being taken advantage of, and being made to live right above the poverty line as indentured servants where they can't afford to quit for fear of not paying their bills; because they're living by the skin of their teeth.

The bosses and the workers could come together if they actually sat down and listened to each other. Sometimes a strike and shutdown is warranted to make sure the bosses hear the workers, forcing them to sit down at the negotiating table. But when both sides do sit down at that proverbial table, and they are willing to talk things out, we must listen and understand where each party is coming from. This way we will hear where everybody is coming from. Basically, it's a lesson of treat somebody like we would like to be treated.

When we listen to somebody and actually hear the words and concepts they convey, we are making the world better.

ACTION MANIFESTO OF A MADMAN FOR GOOD

ENTRY#268

If we sit down to listen to somebody and are hearing what they're saying, is it guaranteed they will do the same with us? Just because we let somebody speak to us about what they feel will better the workplace or society as a whole, doesn't mean when we're conveying our ideas that they won't get immediately disinterested in what we have to say, turning off their hearing receptors and just nodding their heads "uh huh" so as to give us the illusion they're listening, but are really tuning us out and avoiding us.

If nothing in life is guaranteed except death and taxes, then how do we know that our ideas will work?

The thing is we don't know how things will turn out, but that's not why we do them. We don't do things because we know exactly how they will turn out every single time; we do them because we feel strongly about them and because they are the right things to do. Now that said, not everything we do on a daily basis is going to be the right thing to do, we are not perfect specimens, we're only flesh and blood humans. But what we can do is make sure we do the right thing as often as possible.

If we think that workers around us (including ourselves) aren't getting paid enough, we should stand up and say something. If we see a coworker getting harassed by a manager but they are too afraid of saying something for fear of losing their job, we should say something. And most importantly, if we want to change what's around us, we have to change what's around us. We can't just sit around and wait for it to happen.

If we want to prevent the whole system from crashing down on our heads out of fear, greed, profit, and complacency, we must stand up and say what's on our minds and how we're getting taken advantage of. We must be willing to hear the other side, so they hear us. We must never forget why we're attempting to make change. Cause if we forget why, we might as well not even show up at the table at all.

ACTION MANIFESTO OF A MADMAN FOR GOOD

ENTRY#269

Looking ahead, what if we get both sides to talk to each other and compromise on ideas, but not on principles? Can we fix what's really important and what we already agreed on before we started arguing in the first place? What can happen is up to us.

There could be a system that works for most of us instead of against most of us. Minimum wage could keep up with inflation so that somebody could actually get by on it. Health care could be given to everybody that needs it. Education could be available to the masses because the more of us that know about the world around us, the better chance we have to make positive change.

These ideas are all based on having a fair, educated and healthy population that can benefit everyone. We can help the poor by raising them up and giving them the opportunity to make a better life for themselves, where they don't feel like they have to struggle anymore. We can help the middle class by sustaining the gains we've already made and increasing them because the poor would be quickly moving into the middle class. The rich would benefit because their business would be more profitable, their employees more productive, and their opportunities endless of what they could do.

We must stamp out greed with humanity and show these check writers that all of us are human, and deserve a fair shot if we're willing to put the work in. Since the boss is just as human as the worker they're putting down, they must be made to see that by degrading others, they are really degrading themselves. If they want to really better their entire lives and not just their pocket books, they must open their eyes.

ACTION MANIFESTO OF A MADMAN FOR GOOD

ENTRY#270

When confronted by facts to their face, those at the top of the food chain aren't always quick to upset the comfortable system they've set up for themselves. They might be a little hesitant to give up the huge percentages they make above and beyond the people that work for them, and probably feel it's fair because they're the ones behind the business so they deserve the lion's share of the profits; only giving out as least as possible so they can get the most back.

This hesitancy is understandable in the human condition because when we get our selves stuck in a comfortable rut, it seems to make life simple. We fit into a neat and tidy routine that makes getting through the day a lot easier. This is a human condition.

When we are the CEO of a company who makes 400 times what the average worker makes, we completely lose touch. It might have been forever since we had to decide which bill to pay, and which to let sit on the table; which effects society exponentially because it forms the average person's opinion that doesn't know any better. This rut idea is the same as the way people defend themselves, their stuff or what they've worked for whether they make minimum wage or a billion dollars a year.

People don't always want out of comfortable ruts. We must show them that sometimes getting out of ruts can fix the world.

ACTION MANIFESTO OF A MADMAN FOR GOOD

ENTRY#271

If we have all the same needs and wants at our root level, and certain aspects of our journey can be hugely magnified depending on our income or our station in life, how can we plan an attack on the ignorance that still pervades the human condition? How can we arrive at a black and white solution that will make us see everybody within ourselves? Is the idea of looking for a black and white answer a false positive because we know everybody is on a different path?

Life is an interesting journey with a zillion different variables. When fighting for the life and benefit of the workers of industry, and making sure the American dream or even better put, the human dream, is realized by everyone, (no matter where they come from or what they look like) we must never lose sight of why we are struggling. We might see a worker and how bad we feel that they don't get what they deserve, but we must walk in their shoes. We might see the people at the top and how they seem to stomp everything in their path, we must walk in their shoes.

These pairs of shoes might be different sizes, colors, styles and come from different stores, but the point is they're made in the same factories by the same slave labor in the same dirty sweatshop that has been exploiting children for a very long time (and who will continue to exploit kids until we stand up and say something and continue to say something until change happens). We eat from the same pie, let's all grab a piece.

ACTION MANIFESTO OF A MADMAN FOR GOOD

ENTRY#272

When we grab our piece of the pie, not only do we have to remember to grab a napkin for any crumbs that fall, but we also have to make sure the rest of the pie isn't destroyed because of the way we pulled our slice out. We must leave the edges all nice and sharp so when somebody else comes to cut their piece, it's clearly defined and they know what they're getting.

Now I realize that when the average person gets their piece of the economic and societal pie, (which sometimes makes life worth living) it isn't always neat and tidy or clear cut. Sometimes life gets in the way and blurs all its definitions, or one of us disproves the norm and goes our own path by being not only an anomaly, but completely out of the equation; even though a slice might not be cut out neatly, we can be sure that it will be cut out.

We are not perfect beings, no matter how hard we try; it is next to impossible to live completely by our principles. Just the fact that we're making an effort to take a neater piece of pie so everybody else can get their piece and the next person and the next person and so on, just the fact that we are putting an effort forward is half the battle. We have already half won. Looking forward we have to think about how to make it not just more equal and more fair between paycheck earners and paycheck writers, but also how to associate with each other more, and how to see ourselves even more in more situations.

Every time we get into an argument, we should try to see each other in ourselves. When we get a raise, a vacation, promotion or a huge lump of profit that was unexpected, we must see how each person we interact with is going through the same challenges we are; they might have the same heartaches but also some of the same successes. We must see each other in ourselves during good times and bad, because it is this balance that will get us over the hump we're stuck on, the rut we're stuck in, and will help us win more than just half the battle.

ACTION MANIFESTO OF A MADMAN FOR GOOD

ENTRY#273

What is the purpose of joining a protest movement, why would we go out of our way to be a thorn in the side of the government or other authoritative body? Why would we want to rock the boat, and possibly upset the comfortable little rut we think we have set up for ourselves, but really was placed there for us? Why would we want change, it's scary, isn't it?

Sometimes when we go through our routines, nothing seems to be different. We just go through our day, and eat some food, go to work, come home and eat some food, then go to sleep and do it all over again. We might hang out with our family, wife, husband or kids, but otherwise life just seems to run in a cycle without our control or say so.

Bills might be piling up, but we can still pay them, barely. Basically we get stuck in the same cycle, locked into the same job with the same pay that never has a chance for advancement; but we stay there because even though it might not be leading anywhere, it's getting us by, barely.

This is when we have to change something, even if it's small. Just slow down and think if there is anything we might have overlooked because something else needed more immediate action. Open our eyes and we will receive. If we keep our eyes closed and our head down, nothing will ever change. But, if we keep our eyes and our minds open to what's out in the world to better our situation, we can fix our current predicament. We can get past the impossible if it's the right thing to.

Just like Martin Luther King said, "the fight is long but the universe bends towards justice", our daily struggles might seem impossible to get past; but if we keep doing what's best for ourselves and those around us, consciously take advantage of any opportunities that come our way and always keep our eyes and minds open and thinking of what we can do, we can't fail.

Getting together with other like-minded people that feel the same pain and challenges, makes it much more likely that opportunities for major change will not only become more apparent, because more minds are going and putting forth ideas, but because everybody is trying to help everybody.

Sometimes we can fulfill our challenges ourselves, and sometimes we can't. Sometimes a bigger challenge requires a bigger response and a bigger stockpile of conscious energy to be put in, so we can usurp whatever injustice, crime or corruption is going on. This is when movements can help. When the pay check writers and money managers figure out that we're working together because we're now immune to their blinding and soul sucking material power, they become scared because they must now pay attention to us because their comfortable rut is being shaken up. This is when it comes full circle, and we see that we all go through the same challenges and mind games, just coming from different directions and place no matter our financial place in life

We must stay eternally vigilant to what's in front of us and around us if we truly want to make change to our current impossible to change situation. This process is much easier when we work together, and move towards the universal goals that we all feel deep down in our soul is possible. We need this for our personal human development, but more importantly for our collective human evolution.

We will get past the problem of telling ourselves we can't past something because we're too comfortable, feel trapped or don't want to move by asking questions, if we never stop believing. We can do this, but only if we believe we can. The only way we can fail, is if we don't even give ourselves the chance.

ACTION MANIFESTO OF A MADMAN FOR GOOD

ENTRY#274

When is that moment in time or that one event that strikes us so powerfully that we must act? Does talking bring this want on? Does thinking? Or does the simple fact that we think, already put us one step ahead of the rest because we're able to decipher what's real and what's make believe?

The answer to our questions usually come after we have put the time in to study a subject, learn all its ins and outs, can test it, and are able to intellectually deduce what we want answered. There are times however when we know what the question is, whether or not we have asked it, are open and ready to receive the answer, and then it comes to us; sometimes, it falls into our laps without any thought at all. The former happens much more often than the latter, but each can happen at any time, and so we must prepare for everything.

One thing I know for sure is that we only act when we're ready and willing. Sometimes we are forced to act yes, but we won't act nearly as powerfully as we would if we put our full energy and want into an action.

Where is our moment, how can we see it if we don't look or keep our eyes closed?

ACTION MANIFESTO OF A MADMAN FOR GOOD

ENTRY#275

Keeping our eyes open to the world around us, and readying ourselves for change to happen, is how we move forward as a species. Joining together with other like-minded people is how we collectively evolve into a person that can see 360 degrees; and are not only ready for change, but we come to expect it.

We can start a group that talks about a single issue that deals with any number of different rights groups, and put our collective energy forward to achieving those goals. Of course we can do anything, but are we also ready to deal with the people around us? Can we get to together with people that don't agree with us? Can we handle opinions that are different from our own? Is this humanistic discourse the key to the whole megillah?

We must always stay open to what's around us when we start to observe the world, because we are just discovering how everything works. The situation now is the same as it's always been, the only difference is that we're older, have more responsibilities and don't have as big an imagination. The effort we have to put in to making the situation better is more, but we're more informed and more efficient at the same time.

In an age of efficiency and conserving energy (and money for that matter) our time is brutally important. We must spend it in the right way so that we don't end up hating ourselves at the end of the day. We must see the deeper underlying issues that are keeping us from coming together, we must save our energy.

ACTION MANIFESTO OF A MADMAN FOR GOOD

ENTRY#276

How do we save the energy we need to sustain ourselves for the long evolutionary battle ahead? How do we know we're headed in the right direction? How on earth can there be an answer to either of those questions? The reason we must band together instead of fighting for all our own single issues is that there's an underlying current running under them all. Whether they support rights or access, are against discrimination, for peace, for love or for justice, a group is much more powerful and influential when they band together with the underlying issue.

Doesn't it seem easier sometimes if we would just wake up and see that we're fighting for our rights, somebody else is fighting for their rights, and we both have a much better chance at succeeding if we would just come together and fight for rights for everybody? Does that sound crazy? What is more powerful, one person with a mind to change the world, or many people that band together and coalesce their energy to change the world?

We know that we are doing the right thing, when we feel it in the pit of our stomach. That's the hard thing to catch for most of us, it's the same but different at the same time. We will know it when it happens, if we are paying attention.

ACTION MANIFESTO OF A MADMAN FOR GOOD

ENTRY#277

Paying attention, being conscious or being in the moment, (whatever we want to call it) is the reason we as a people see there are problems with society in the first place.

Sometimes when we as a people group together for a collective good or to fight for something we all know is right, there will be other groups of people that want to end our operations because they see it as threatening what they're trying to do. We have to realize this can't stop us from fighting for what's right. If we're too scared to even put our feet on the ground for something that we know in our heart is right, how can we ever expect to achieve our dreams?

We must not be scared to join a group, or be intimidated out of getting together with other individuals to collectively do some good work for humanity. We must never back down from what's in our heart. This is the hard part to explain because there really is no black and white cure-all answer to what's in all of our hearts. But, if we have good intentions, are ready to go out and take on the paycheck writers and their governmental overlords (or under lords depending on how we look at it), we will have much better luck if we open our eyes and take a look around.

ACTION MANIFESTO OF A MADMAN FOR GOOD

ENTRY#278

Am I crazy to think that everybody wants to positively change the world? Am I deranged to think that people will even be able to see past their own baggage and demons to see what's truly best for them and everybody around them? Is the fact that I believe in people's good nature, and have the ability to see that their basic needs are the same as their neighbors prove I need to be committed?

I may have gone off the deep end with that last line of questioning, but it's true. Do we as a people have what it takes to affect the change that we all feel? Can we get past any bullshit gridlock and manufactured crisis so we can get to the heart of the issue, which again has to deal with everything we learned in kindergarten?

The point is I know I am an eternal optimist, who will always try taking a positive view of the world with an eye to positively change what's around us, because it's all I know how to do. I also realize there are a lot of pessimistic people out there that take a negative view of the world and always play devil's advocate (even when they don't care what they are talking about). We will unite when we realize that we aren't two different coins, we are two sides of the same coin.

We will be able to join together to fight for what's right when we realize that the world doesn't revolve around us, it revolves around everybody and everything.

ACTION MANIFESTO OF A MADMAN FOR GOOD

ENTRY#279

When we're fighting for progress and know how we can all come together around what we already agree on, what do we do when we come up against somebody that thinks we're nuts, or at the very least thinks we're completely wrong and have the whole thing backwards? Are they the enemies of progress because they are impeding our path? Are we the enemies of progress because we are trying to proselytize our path to them? Or is there a reason we were brought together in the first place, which might be to help each other find a middle path that works equally for all because deep down we are all the same?

When we're moving forward and see and feel the energy that propels the human race forward, does everybody else see it the same way? Maybe the trick is knowing that we all arrive at our present circumstances from different paths, backgrounds and experiences, and remembering we all have our challenges to get through. Once we've arrived at this point, to have a chance to move forward we have to see where we come together, where we can relate on a human level. This point of coming together is there, we just have to wake up to it.

We might all seem different, like we're all coming from different places so how could we ever agree. But, if we just slow down and look at the fact that we are all human, we will see we all want to feel love, want to be safe, and deep down (whether we want to admit it or not) want peace for the world so all of its inhabitants can live freely and not under threat of destruction.

If we want to actually move forward and not keep getting stuck in the same muck that we've been mired in for generations, we have to do something different, and we have to change. This change does not have to be scary, anxiety filled and surrounded by the outlook of doom because everything and everybody around us seems to be telling us that there is no possible way out. There will always be those of us out there that say the world is going to keep getting worse, causing people to keep getting imbedded in separate camps and becoming more polarized as the days go by.

This change can be welcoming, loving, filled with our hopes and dreams for equality, justice, peace, love and fairness. We have to ask ourselves what we really want. Let the fog drift away and see what happens. Do we really want to keep fighting forever? Are we waiting for the rapture to come lift us up and destroy our enemies? Or are we at the right moment of time to understand the stakes of not coming together, that we can come together and relate to each other if we just listen and see everybody as ourselves. We must realize that because we have a lot more in common than we don't have in common, it's a lot easier to come together than we might think. We just have to slow down and really listen.

ACTION MANIFESTO OF A MADMAN FOR GOOD

ENTRY#280

There is a time and a place when each of us comes to realize the true power we have, when all the things in life that confused us before become clearer; the difficult part comes when we try to figure out when, because there is no black and white answer for any of us. Since we're all unique snowflakes as some like to say, there is a different point in all of our lives when suddenly a light bulb goes off in our heads and we think, oh yeah, that's what I'm supposed to be doing. How do we know when that power arrives or what exactly it is?

Well my friends, I'm here to tell you that even though you've probably heard "you'll just know" plenty of times, it still rings true. When things become clear is when they become clear. And although that might not mean anything at the moment, just wait. Wait for that moment to happen. Now I'm not talking about waiting in the traditional sense. I'm talking about staying open to all of life's possibilities, ready to accept them without using force, and feeling the love and beauty in the world that is all around us. Once we are able to do this, we will see that our moment has come.

ACTION MANIFESTO OF A MADMAN FOR GOOD

ENTRY#281

With so much going on in our everyday lives from work, worrying about the bills, the family, the kids, putting food on the table, to how am I going to make a real mark on society for the better, it can be hard to slow down and think deeply about what's actually happening around us. It takes practice to make time for ourselves, to say that our time is valuable enough to spend it on our own well-being; it is something we must do so we can evolve.

Well some might say, why would I care about evolving, isn't that some kind of hippy talk? Is it hippy talk to speak about wanting all of us to have a fair shot if we're willing to work towards something we believe in? Is it hippy talk to say that we want to take care of the earth so it continues to support us so that our great great-great-great grandchildren still know the beauty and joy that we can feel every day (that is if we are open and ready to accept it)?

There are many distractions in life, some that are imposed from the outside, and some that are imposed from within us. We must not get in the way of doing what our brains tell us to do, but most importantly what our hearts tells us to do. Knowing about the balance between the two is what will really make the difference.

ACTION MANIFESTO OF A MADMAN FOR GOOD

ENTRY#282

Finding the balance between what our brains tell us to do and what our hearts feel we must do can be a little tricky. On the one hand, we know there are certain responsibilities we must meet to survive in the adult world; we must have a job, pay our bills, have a place to live, we must raise a family and be a good wife or husband if we have one. We must also remember to have fun, go out and take a long walk on a beautiful day, enjoy the nature that's around or the other beauty that may be hiding in plain sight just waiting to be observed. We must love and feel love in return so we can wake up in the morning and have motivation to go through our day, while trying to make the world a better place.

Balancing our routine is helpful when we try to find time to fit everything into a schedule. What do we have time for, and when can we cram in some "me time" when we aren't too tired or the kids aren't screaming at us for something?

If we don't see that figuring our life out, (where it's heading and where we would like it to head) as important enough to spend time on, life will swallow up whatever time we thought we had, and make us realize that balance might never happen; this is a type of self-imposed distraction that will stop us in our tracks.

If we do the make the time for self-reflection, and take five minutes to think about what's going on around us, (not just what's happening right in front of our face) those times when we have to use our brain won't seem so daunting. We can have everything in life that we deserve as human beings, we just have to slow down long enough to realize that everybody does also. We will all get there when we are ready to receive it.

ACTION MANIFESTO OF A MADMAN FOR GOOD

ENTRY#283

Somebody might come up and ask, well, how do I know when I'm on my path? When am I headed I the right direction?

There is no blue print for the path all of us should take in life, (nor should there be) there is just a feeling of gratitude and love that can be hard to put into words. It's like this overwhelming sensation of warmth and love that is all around us making us know that we're an active being in this world; we are seeing ourselves alongside everybody else in the pursuit of what's real.

Even though we're all pursuing happiness and might take completely different paths to get there, the point is that we will get there. We don't know how and we don't know when, but we will get there. This isn't blind faith, this is knowing that things will work out because not only can we picture them, but we can feel them as well.

Try it, think about what's around us right now, see the beauty that is really there, not just what's in front of us. Can we feel it?

ACTION MANIFESTO OF A MADMAN FOR GOOD

ENTRY#284

What is the problem with knowing? Is there an issue with the facts that one of us knows in our heart? If one of us has a truth and another one of us has a truth, how do we reconcile that when we come up against each other either in battle or conversation?

Maybe the answer is just listening to what the other side has to say, and knowing that somebody else's truth shouldn't be argued. Whichever side that knows what the important conversation is, is the side that's conscious of what's going on in front of them, instead of what they think is going on.

We get so caught up in rhetoric, propaganda so thick it's impossible to know what either side is really trying to say, let alone what they really want. This is when it's important to open our hearts, minds and most importantly our ears to what's happening all around us. It might be something we thought we lost. It might be something that's hiding. It might be something that has been there the whole time that we just refused to see.

ACTION MANIFESTO OF A MADMAN FOR GOOD

ENTRY#285

What happens when we don't listen to what's happening and we just talk over it? Do we drown out whatever messages we might have received? Was there something that we're supposed to do or a place we were supposed to be, but because of self-distraction (and a pre-conceived notion of knowing what the world is like without ever experiencing it) we don't listen?

Listening and not just hearing is a learned trait that is harder for some than it is for others. We have to remember that if we're better listeners than somebody else and know what's going on, we must never ridicule them and put them down for it, which will just push them further away. The same goes for those of us that don't know what's going on. When we interact with somebody that professes to know all sorts of information we can't insult and put them down for knowing and paying attention.

The hard part is finding out that each of these sides could be hiding their true identities. The "know it alls" might really be parroting something they heard because they think it's too hard to look deeply into something.

The "know nothings" might be the ones that know what's going on, but choose not to throw it in people's faces. The key to figuring out which is which, is listening not just hearing; feeling not just thinking. When the truth comes along, we will know it if we pay attention.

ACTION MANIFESTO OF A MADMAN FOR GOOD

ENTRY#286

There has to be a point of agreement if there is going to be a point of contact, right? What's the point of having contact if there is going to be no agreement? How do we expect to ever get past historical battles for land and treasure, and see that the people that we're really fighting against are ourselves? When will we get to the point where we realize that we are no better than the person next to us? All we have to do to succeed in this world is be open to possibilities, keep love in our hearts, and make sure that we're listening to messages that we're supposed to receive, whether they come from our heart, mind or from our environment.

We must ask ourselves if we really want to get past some of the stuff that we've been fighting over, but never seem to get anywhere. Are we satisfied with fighting the same old battles over and over again while expecting different results? Are we able to live in a world that is completely dominated by one sided thinking, where the creative mind and anything else that upsets the status quo is harshly destroyed for being the one thing that rocks the boat, making everybody think there might be a better way?

There might be a better way of doing things huh? You mean what one side is telling me isn't the omniscient truth? We must stay open or we won't have to worry about the robots taking over, we will become them ourselves.

ACTION MANIFESTO OF A MADMAN FOR GOOD

ENTRY#287

Robots taking over the planet always seemed like the funniest metaphor to me. On one side a mass intelligence apparatus that is all knowing and all powerful controls every move and action of the population. The former masters in turn fall into the slavery pit of never ending despair, with the thought that they will never escape because they not only designed the pit, but they dug it as well.

This one has many layers to it. We have the oppressed rising to throw off the oppressor. We have the corporate machine getting so big that it implodes and eats itself from the inside out by the very thing they thought would never happen; but they forgot about the human greed factor and how there is never enough. Ever heard the business saying that if you aren't growing you're dying? These people will be the first people to be taken over by the robots.

But seriously, we have to pay attention folks, I can't stress this enough. We have to see what's going on around us and think about the ramifications of what our actions and creations will be. If we don't, we are no better than the robots waiting to take over our living room. Watch out, a robot might come get us if we don't think. I'm not talking about the thinking that creates the robot; I'm talking about the thoughts that will raise consciousness of the entire planet to a level where heaven and earth merge, and everything is as it should be.

We have the ability to move forward towards whatever future we want, we just have to ask ourselves, what would we rather live with?

ACTION MANIFESTO OF MADMAN FOR GOOD

ENTRY#288

We touched on robots, now let's touch on dinosaurs; I'm not talking about the tyrannosaurus and the brontosaurus, I'm talking about the people that walk among us that are stuck in a way of thinking that is blocking progress. I'm not talking about the older generation in terms of age, but way of thinking.

Dinosaurs ruled the earth for a long time. Well, they didn't really rule the earth, they were just the biggest things walking around and nothing could destroy them except a big asteroid or explosion. Is this the same thing that has to happen for dinosaur thinking to go the way of the dodo and just go extinct? Is it even possible for it to ever disappear?

If we're trying to achieve a balance in life, don't we need a point of reference for all the good things we're doing to know if they're good or not? Is this just what we're telling ourselves? What we tell ourselves has a very powerful effect in the way we carry ourselves, not only in our daily life, but as a citizen of the world. We can be negative or we can be positive.

We can be resistant to change and fight tooth and nail to keep everything like it was at time of the dinosaurs, or we can adapt and change with the time because the universe always bends towards justice. We can tell ourselves just about anything. What matters is moving forward with positivity, not backwards with hate.

ACTION MANIFESTO OF A MADMAN FOR GOOD

ENTRY#289

When the sun is in our face it can feel like the pressure is on to hurry up and get where we want to be and where other people think we should be. The burning rays feel like they can pierce through our soul like a thousand little daggers if we let it get ahold of what's good and beautiful about us. Or do they? Do they feel like something burning through our soul, something that adds to the warmth of our soul, or something that is to our detriment by preventing us from seeing? Is the sun shining a light on something and bringing it to our attention for closer observation?

We will never know what's right in front of us unless we take a look. We will never know what sounds are there if we don't open our ears. But most importantly, (and this includes everybody regardless of hearing and sight ability) we will never know what we are supposed to receive if we don't open our souls.

This doesn't mean let anybody do anything they want to us because we're open and have to experience everything to make sure we don't miss anything. It just means that we're open to everything, so we see everything. When we see everything, we have to decide what is good, what is bad, what is for our highest good and what isn't.

When the sun is shining in our eyes, whether it is at the beginning, middle or the end of the day, just remember to always respect the light that's shining, and remember its purpose, and our own.

ACTION MANIFESTO OF A MADMAN FOR GOOD

ENTRY#290

When the sun sets and dips over the horizon, is it the end of the road of discovery? Does it disappear because our brains can only hold so much information at one time, not wanting to overload us with too much crap in one sitting? Or is it just the end of one experience and the beginning of another possibly even more fulfilling one?

I guess most of this comes down to choice. Do we want to put a negative spin on something that is happening or a positive spin? Do or should we put a spin on something at all? Is putting a spin on something just a way of figuring out the world when it all seems like chaos, or is it just a way of confusing ourselves to keep our minds spinning? Or is it just a way to ignore, blind and distract ourselves so we don't have to face what's really going on in front of us?

The only way we will get past these questions is if we start thinking about them. We only have to intend to do them to start the flow of consciousness. When we start thinking about bigger questions it might be hard the first time, especially if we haven't done it much before; but that is where intent comes in.

If we're having a hard time thinking deeply about something, we must stop and ask ourselves why we're having such a hard time with it, and if it's the best use of our time. When the sun sets, it can bring up all kinds of things. It can bring the darkness of the night, or the planning of a new day.

ACTION MANIFESTO OF A MADMAN FOR GOOD

ENTRY#291

There is only so much light in the day, some of us might think there is only so much love in our hearts as well. What we have to ask ourselves is do we really think that is true because we've heard people say it, or because we actually believe it? Is there a time when we can be filled up with love too much, or when we can't think past a certain point because we haven't been guided and taught to think for ourselves?

Sometimes we have to forge our own path in life. Sometimes what the world, society, and sometimes even what our friends and family was has to be set aside so we can pursue what we know in our hearts to be the right thing to do.

It would be so easy in this book, if I could just tell you all what to do and how to live. But that is not what I'm here for, and I definitely don't profess to know everything, or I wouldn't have to write a book like this in the first place. I am here figuring things out just like you. And I know now that the time has come to put some of my thoughts on paper so the world can see what's rolling around in my brain; that I really, truly and authentically want to change the world for the better and want to help us evolve. The only way I know how to do that is to spread as much love as I can to everybody and everything I come into contact with, and also what I haven't come into contact with yet, or might not ever. All I'm saying is thinking outside the box has helped me; it might help you as well. With the amount of time we have, what will we think about?

ACTION MANIFESTO OF A MADMAN FOR GOOD

ENTRY#292

The ending of the day physically doesn't have to be the end of the day mentally. Just because the light of the sun has gone away, doesn't mean the light of our heart, soul and mind has gone away. Just because a physical representation of beauty is standing in front of us and presenting all its glory, doesn't mean it's not easily accessible every day. Once we have seen the true beauty of the world, we can relive it and at any moment we want; we can feed the need by just remembering what it looked like. Then when we remember what it looked like, we can remember what it felt like. When we remember what it felt like we are right back in it. When we are right back in it, we are right back where we are supposed to be because as we will see through experience, it is where we were always meant to be.

The ending of our output, might only be the start of another input, we have to decide for ourselves which one it is. Sure we could have somebody else tell us what they think it is, but all they are going to do is give their interpretation of what they think the next step is. What we need for ourselves and for the planet is to think critically. It sounds so simple right, think. Just think. I'm not talking about over analyzing, (because that can be a very distractive force on its own) I'm referring to paying attention to our intuitions and what we feel is the right thing to do. This sounds like a difficult task, but gets much easier almost normal the more we do it. So at the end of the day don't cry and don't worry, be happy.

ACTION MANIFESTO OF A MADMAN FOR GOOD

ENTRY#293

Motivation can be a hard thing to receive or hold onto, (let alone to create ourselves) especially when we don't have anything around willing or able to be of any assistance. Why do we seem to want to strive more and even talk about it from time to time, but fail to get off our couch to do anything about it?

There is a solution however. The answer to our being, staying or getting motivated is to be happy. If we don't know how to make ourselves happy, we either need some serious help, or more likely we just need a little reminder of what used to make us happy; what brings us the most joy. It could be a happy memory about us learning to ride our bike, or walking down the street for an ice cream cone, or hanging out with some friends at a BBQ.

Remembering what makes us happy is only the first step however (it is simply a jumping off point to our consciousness). The next step is remembering how we felt during those happy moments, which is what can bring the real power.

ACTION MANIFESTO OF A MADMAN FOR GOOD

ENTRY#294

Are the hidden answers to the universe really as simple as thinking deeply enough about what we actually see right in front of us, and to remember that everybody else on the planet is trying to do the same thing even if they don't realize it yet?

We have all heard talking heads endlessly drone on about how we just have to think about situations critically, about the parties involved and how their human reaction might be the same as ours if the roles were reversed. Wait a minute, most of them don't talk about that stuff, and maybe that's part of the problem, more on that later.

However it gets done, and whoever said to think critically first doesn't matter in the end, only the act itself of thinking critically about a situation matters. If there is a positive result from us actually thinking about what's going on right under our nose, it won't matter where the inspiration came from.

While just thinking critically might work for a while, for us to be able to sustain it for any length of time, we will not only have to know where it comes from, but also how to produce it at will.

ACTION MANIFESTO OF A MADMAN FOR GOOD

ENTRY#295

If the way to motivate ourselves is to be happy by remembering happy moments and what they felt like, what's after that? This is some sort of process right?

Maybe the answer to all the problems we know lies in the unknown. I know that sounds like some elitist know it all answer, but I assure you that is not its intent.

We have to go into the unknown and not be afraid of it; that way when an opportunity arises to better ourselves and the world around us, we are in a great position to do something about it.

Maybe the next step is to simply remember what love feels like. We can raise our energy by putting ourselves in a positive space, and sharing it with everybody we come into contact with; they can feed off of it, and spread it to everybody they come into contact with. This simple act could be enough to bring love into our collective lives, which allows us to share it with others. Love fills up our energy from those we touch, which we in turn give right back to them. And the never ending cycle of love and harmony is on its way.

There are many big questions, what is the next step, what is the next adventure, what is the next opportunity? We can be sure that the only way we will retain the information we receive when we come across it, is to hear. We have to listen and then hear what's going on around us, or we might miss what we've always been looking for.

ACTION MANIFESTO OF A MADMAN FOR GOOD

ENTRY#296

Blades of grass on the front lawn gently swaying in the breeze might be able to bring us all the peace we will ever need. Maybe it's the smell of a jasmine flower in bloom that wafts its way into our nostrils and down into our soul. Maybe it's simply the act of realizing we still have the ability to surprise ourselves, and can shake off distractions and pre-conditions we've placed on ourselves whether we know it or not.

Everybody wants to find peace because it's a pretty human emotion right? Every single one of us on this precious planet wants to find peace and experience it for as long as we can, we know that right?

We can always find peace in the overwhelming sense of joy and happiness that surrounds us, whether it's looking out at the water, a tree, a beach, a yard, a living room, an office building in the middle of an urban jungle or anything in between.

Once we realize that peace and happiness is all around us, all we have to do is just tap into it; once we do we will find that it has unlimited refills once we remember how to twist the knob.

ACTION MANIFESTO OF MADMAN FOR GOOD

ENTRY#297

When somebody says, "I don't care which way the wind blows, it doesn't really matter to me," what do they mean? I don't mean if they are the lead singer of queen.

Does it just mean doing your own thing, no matter what anybody else says? Does it mean having enough confidence to carry on amidst adversity no matter what happens, because you know you're doing the right thing? Or does it mean that it's damn cold outside and its looks really sunny and nice, but when we step out there, it's freezing?

Maybe the answer to why things matter or don't matter to us lies in somebody whose memory left us long ago. Maybe the answer lies within our souls, and we only have to ask ourselves in a truthful and loving manner. Maybe it simply means we all have a purpose (I think I have found mine and I am striving toward it). Since whatever society thinks is okay and acceptable is going to change no matter what happens to us, we must move forward with what we think is right for our soul.

Sometimes the only way to find answers is a little introspection.

ACTION MANIFESTO OF A MADMAN FOR GOOD

ENTRY#298

I love the earth and its entire people, I really do. This might sound a little weird coming right at the beginning of some writing, but there it is. "I felt like saying it" is what writing is all about, putting down what you're thinking.

What I'm trying to say is that I feel an overwhelming sense of love and gratitude towards mankind, the earth, all beings and organisms living now, all that have lived in the past and the ones that will live in the future. This is something that comes from practice, definitely not something that happens overnight, (but maybe the thing I've been missing, is that it can happen instantly).

I think the reason great things happen when we least expect them is because of just that, we aren't expecting them. We don't have any pre conceived notions about what might happen and we can't gauge how we are going to feel. We can't pattern the best response to great things happening; all we can do is completely open up to the experience.

Staying open, willing and able to receive is something that comes when we feel the beauty of the earth; we know it's there to help make our lives worth living. We must realize it is never too late to see beauty, because it will always be there.

What we have to remember is that our remembering powers are a finite resource; which is a place we have to get to if we want to find peace. And like I said in my last piece, we want peace, right?

ACTION MANIFESTO OF A MADMAN FOR GOOD

ENTRY#299

Having a picnic on a sunny day can be one of the most rewarding experiences we could have. Maybe you are saying right now this guy has got it right, or maybe you're saying I don't like picnics and I don't know why this guy would be talking about them in the first place. The reason I bring them up is because picnics are one of my favorite metaphors for the way we can interact with nature, and give us the ability to really find ourselves.

First of all, this picnic can involve food in a basket or in a bag, or no food or basket at all; it could just involve sitting outside on a beautiful day and breathing in the beauty of the world that is waiting for us to grab hold. We have the power to realize that we can be happy, we can feel love. The real love we are searching for is inside ourselves.

The real picnic happens when we step outside of ourselves and think about our situation and how we feel about it. Remember the simple fact of thinking, just thinking.

The point is that once we open that door of what's actually happening and not just blindly go along, we have to be prepared for not only the positive and happiness, but also the negative and unhappiness. We just have to ask ourselves, what would we rather see?

ACTION MANIFESTO OF A MADMAN FOR GOOD

ENTRY#300

Is diplomacy a good thing? Is talking to our friends and enemies always the way to go, whether they're in our personal, familial, political or spiritual lives? Is finding what the other side is thinking the way to get past a generations old conflict like the flip of a switch? If two parties that have been fighting over the same piece of land forever could get past their differences just by hearing what the other side has to say (instead of just parroting the same old lines that have become clichés), will they do it? Can or will they have the strength? This is a question that I'm sure if we had the answer, we probably would have fixed the problem by now.

I must harken back to the fact that whether it be Catholics and Protestants, Muslims and Jews, Muslims and Christians, Buddhists and Hindus, no matter what the battle or history might be, they can all be solved with tolerance, acceptance and love (it's the only reason that these battles happen in the first place, getting back at the other side because the other side struck first). Is the cycle of revenge really so easy as to end with a simple thought?

The only way to do that is to talk to one another. We never know what we could find out, especially if we come from a place of respect and love.

ACTION MANIFESTO OF MADMAN FOR GOOD

ENTRY#301

If we want to fight the good fight, but want to come together at the same time because we know it will end the fighting, how do we balance the two? How do we balance the idea of standing up for what we believe in with the idea of standing beside our brothers and sisters? How do we bring into our heart the idea that the only way to keep moving forward and staying in a positive direction is to figure out the problem, no matter how it hard it is?

We seem so far away from our consciousness potential right now, that as a society it would seem like we will never get back on track. The tricky part though is not only do we have the power to get back on track, we have always had the power and just have to remember what's important to us. Our well-being is pretty similar to the person standing next to us, and once we realize that, things will get easier; it might seem euphoric at first, but the more we practice, the more normal it seems.

It's as though we must build up our tolerance for peace so high that it's not special anymore, it's just something we do.

ACTION MANIFESTO OF A MADMAN FOR GOOD

ENTRY#302

Does keeping love in our hearts so we can move forward in a positive and conscious manner cause us to notice everything around us? Do we want to only emit good energy because that is all that our bodies can or will absorb? There are a number of groups (whether they be religious or secular) that believe by moving forward with joy and a feeling of knowing exactly where we're at, our purpose will be revealed to us.

There is something that runs through all groups, peoples, beings, organisms and all unknowns; they want to make life better for themselves and whoever is close to them. This has always been an admirable trait, and should be something all of us try to live by on a daily basis. We begin to see that things can be even better than that when we realize all of us think that way. Yeah, we might take different paths to get there, they might even be completely opposite; the point is that we get there if we have the intent. Purposely bettering ourselves and those we affect (which is technically everybody and everything) is half of the path forward. I realize that it can be hard to get to that point. All we have to do to move from positive intent into positive action is to feel and know it ourselves. Once we prove it to ourselves, we can prove it to everybody else.

ACTION MANIFESTO OF A MADMAN FOR GOOD

ENTRY#303

As we roll through life and pick up the various connections that are supposed to cross our path, we pick up understanding. This understanding is something that can't be taught in school, lectured about in an auditorium or heard about by walking by the water cooler on the way to our desk.

What makes us human and want to strive for more is something we pick up through experiences, and some of us have had admittedly more than others. But just because we may have had fewer experiences, doesn't mean they were any less meaningful.

These experiences, these "moments" are the little things that make up our life. I know I might have said it before but I feel like saying it again, when somebody says don't sweat the small stuff, pay attention to the bigger picture, it's only about half the message.

The other half is that it's the little things that make up life, they create the bigger picture. I think the key is to acknowledge these moments, get the message they are trying to convey and then let them go.

We shouldn't hang on to them but keep them in our memory banks to pull from whenever we need a boost;

that is how we keep ourselves open to new and exciting experiences, and how we stay open and clear.

Sometimes to bring in the new we have to clear out the old.

ACTION MANIFESTO OF A MADMAN FOR GOOD

ENTRY#304

How do we clear out the old and figure out what doesn't serve us anymore? How do we get rid of what served an admittedly important purpose at one time, but no longer carries the same meaning? How do we know what is for our highest good, is it something that creates a warm and loving feeling that raises our energy whenever we come into contact with it?

Is there something in the air that makes us want to be something more than what we are at the present moment? How can we evolve?

There is a difference between wanting to be more than we are and actually being something better. One has to do with changing ourselves into something we aren't, and the other has to do with improving the existing model. Do we want to change or just improve? Do we see ourselves as unimportant or just working toward something that hasn't come to fruition yet?

Well, as the old saying goes, there is no there, there. Life is all about the journey. The moment we find happiness within ourselves and can feel the gratitude that runs through our veins on a 24-7 basis, (if we want it to or not) we will see the path forward.

We need to be happy and grateful for what we have. Gratitude comes with feeling love and beauty in our hearts whatever our given situation. We can evolve, we can improve, we can do it.

ACTION MANIFESTO OF A MADMAN FOR GOOD

ENTRY#305

We can come together around the same idea or wavelength no matter what our background, religion, ethnicity, culture, where we came from, what we look like, who we love, where we've been and where we are going. It can be very difficult trying to figure out where the hell we are on this earth while still trying to define ourselves (maybe we don't believe in definitions at all). There is a single unifying force that can bring everything together, which has worked in the past and could be and probably should be covered in all the top scientific journals, if there actually was a way to quantify it.

I'm not talking about some new religion that is trying to be better than all the rest, or some cult where people join and just blindly follow whatever the leader says. I'm not even talking about evil super villains that want to take over the world and destroy everything on their way to enslaving humanity and sucking up all of its resources.

What I am talking about is love. Love is the only unifying force that brings all the world's problems, historical struggles and other long standing difficulties to a grinding halt. It might take over night or it might take years to sink in. Love can takeover instantly like a light bulb popping on when we've had a brainstorm. Sometimes good things take time, and sometimes great things happen all at once.

ACTION MANIFESTO OF A MADMAN FOR GOOD

ENTRY#306

How do we find love, how do we feel love, how do we allow love to enter the frontal cortex of our brains and then down into our heart so we feel the warmth of its embrace? Is there a unifying answer of how we find love or are we just twisting out here in the wind like a flag on a windy day?

When the Beatles said "all you really need is love", they were correct, in the beginning. Love is really all we need to begin our journey. We can then carry that love with us wherever we go, engaging and meeting lots of people along the way that are trying to find their path just like us; we see what lies ahead. It's like having a good foundation that we can build from. We can't build a sturdy house on top of something that isn't stable and isn't going to support the weight of all the things put on top of it. We must start with love, and then move forward. We always use love as a means of support because it is the motivation that not only keeps us striving for more during our journey, but also makes life worth living.

We start with love, so we can use it along the way. We give love and we take love amidst a big cycle; and as long as we contribute into it, we will be able to have all we need. It's like when everybody throws in for a pizza, if we don't pay our share, we won't get a slice.

ACTION MANIFESTO OF A MADMAN FOR GOOD

ENTRY#307

We can find love and everything else we need for our journey by opening our eyes and looking around, outside and within our own minds. We have the tools and the power we need within us at all times.

Once we get started, there is no going back; it's like once we know something, we can't un know it. Once we hear that governments are asserting the right to kill anybody at random (for reasons they deem vital to their security), we begin looking at the world a little differently. Once we hear that money is the root of all evil, we will see how it permeates governments, corporatism and all public life to the point where it's the main motivation to stomp on the other guy if it means getting ahead.

Whatever life experiences we have, and realizations we undergo makes up the way we think; we always have the power to use it for something positive. Whatever happens to us, whatever we find out, there is always something positive we can pull from it if we just look.

We might discover it comes down to our choice, how do we want to use the information? Do we want to let it destroy us, or do we want to let it lift us up?

ACTION MANIFESTO OF A MADMAN FOR GOOD

ENTRY#308

Life does seem to come down to choices. What are we going to do today? What are we going to eat, where or from what source? What are we going to do at work, do we work at all or do we play? What do we feel like we have time for? What do we do when part of us says we should put our head down and not rock the boat, and the other part says we should stand up and not only fight for what we believe in, but what we think is right?

The tricky part is when we realize that what we believe in might not always lead us to the right actions or thoughts. We have to pay attention to not only the messages that we get from outside sources, but also the ones we put into our own head as well.

Of course, the choice might be as simple as do we want to be happy with what we have, or are we going to be sad and upset about what we don't? Are we going to do what tears us down and makes our energy plummet, or are we going to do what builds us up and gives us the positive energy to do what we didn't think possible.

We have a choice, we always have and we always will.

ACTION MANIFESTO OF MADMAN FOR GOOD

ENTRY#309

Do we really know what the next few days are going to bring, does anybody? Are there people out there that can positively say for a fact what's going to happen in the day that lies ahead, or the next few, or the next week?

Sometimes life can be confusing and everything can seem like its coming at us all at once with no way to stop it. Sometimes life can seem like it's moving so slow that the slug slithering on the ground next to us will make it farther ahead than us.

Being open and ready to receive is always the key. If we have no idea if life is too fast or too slow, (it's just kind of blaaah) we must stay open and breathe in the beauty all around us just waiting to be observed and paid attention to. Sometimes we can be sitting there while some guy talks way too loud on his cell phone and can be totally annoying. Then he starts talking about his kids first birthday and how cute, smart and fast learning they are, and how he has this extremely cute video of his kid trying to put his hat on.

Anything out there can bring beauty, love and peace. We just have to be vigilantly observant.

ACTION MANIFESTO OF A MADMAN FOR GOOD

ENTRY#310

Numbers can cause a lot of trouble, pain and heart ache if they are directed in the wrong way. The same can be said for symbols that are used to portray what something represents.

If a symbol represents a group of people that preach hate and violence against certain people, it can conjure up a strong image in our mind. If that same symbol is used by a group that preaches love and accepts we're all the same basic people striving in the same direction (but from different paths), it can conjure up something totally different, even though it might be the same symbol.

Signs, numbers, decals or seals (whatever the term that's used) are a way to represent for somebody what they can use for their own ends. The idea is to not believe in the symbol, but in what the groups are using it for. We have to decide, it is our choice.

ACTION MANIFESTO OF MADMAN FOR GOOD

ENTRY#311

Sports can be a good way to get out some energy, aggression, and have some healthy competition. For some of us it can be a way to show dominance over the other players and how great we are and how stupid and crappy they are. It can be viewed as something that is used to promote violence with constant hitting and crashing into each other which is just the type of thing that will tear us apart.

There are a lot of different things we could think about a lot of different subjects. What our intent is and what we feel in our hearts is what really matters. Then comes the empathy for each other that we feel and how comments can hurt us even though we might not mean them, and vice versa.

The interesting parts of life happen when we stay centered in the truth of what we're doing, and are open to all outside stimuli. We push out the bad and keep the good, but we always pay attention to what's actually happening in front of our face.

Sports can be good for many things, but what can't be denied by either side is they bring all types of people together, regardless of where they came from.

Sports haven't always been great, and have a lot of room to still improve; they are but one avenue we can use to figure out more about what's in our soul and what we're made of.

ACTION MANIFESTO OF A MADMAN FOR GOOD

ENTRY#312

Being a bird must be one of the most freeing things anyone could experience; flying around the sky eating and pooping wherever and whenever we felt like it, while at the same time squawking at the hot chick next to us that's looking at us like she is interested. There are also predators of all sorts, bigger birds, hunters on the ground, airplanes, etc. Whatever the case may be, nothing is totally freeing, it just depends on how we look at it and what we make out of the experience.

Some people may look up at the sky and see birds flying over their head and think, "those things are so stupid, and probably don't even know I'm down here, somebody is totally going to shoot them and I hope they do". They might be that cruel or not, who knows. I actually see the opposite and how majestic and amazing they are, the amount of combined energy it takes to fly together for long distances every day and to not get lost when they don't have any critical thinking skills is unreal.

Whether we're looking up at the sky and see a bird, a plane, or if we're lucky enough to see superman, we're guaranteed to all see something different; as it is with all other aspects of life, including, what our families should be like and what kinds of politicians and governments we want. Many of us want different things, and that's okay.

There are some basic things that are the same for us, we use this original idea combined with life experience to form our own way. That's why when we look up at the sky we might all think of a different meaning for the birds, but we can still agree they're birds and they sparked our thought and our differing opinions in the first place. It's important that we feel and know what makes us want to strive for more.

ACTION MANIFESTO OF A MADMAN FOR GOOD

ENTRY#313

Whether we're sitting in a parking lot looking at the back of a bunch of cars, or we're chasing our kid who is enjoying the beauty of discovering life, we all come from the same heart and soul connection, something bigger inside ourselves that we all must figure out our own way to tap into it.

It doesn't matter what we're doing, there is the possibility for coincidence, synchronicity or a myriad of different signs that will light the path we're supposed to take (if we only pay attention and slow down long enough to hear what it's trying to tell us). Our path might appear when we're least expecting it; we might be thinking about it, or we expect something to happen because we can picture it and don't know what, where, when or even how, but we do know why.

Things happen for a reason, sometimes we know them but a lot of times we don't. If we are open and willing to see what's out there, then we will not only begin to figure things out, but we will never be alone.

ACTION MANIFESTO OF A MADMAN FOR GOOD

ENTRY#314

It is impossible to arrive at our goals instantly, no matter how hard we try to moan and complain. We must put the work in to make our goals and our dreams happen. We must not sit around and wait for a magic bean to fall into our laps that will fix the problems we know about (and could fix if we only focused). We must take action and realize that there are steps that need to be taken in preparation, so we can ready ourselves for the long road ahead. It will be hard work but it will be worth it.

Let me say that I am probably using the wrong word when I say work. Once we realize that what we're taking part in is for our own benefit as well as the rest of humanity, it won't seem so much like work, it will just seem like something we must do, because it makes us happy not only while we are doing it, but afterwards as well.

We need to take the time to count our blessings, be grateful for everything we have, and always remember to pay it forward. These are only some of the ways that we begin to "work".

ACTION MANIFESTO OF A MADMAN FOR GOOD

ENTRY#315

Doing guess work, figuring out what works and what doesn't is a constant of life that will always happen, it also has the potential to help us find what we're looking for (or at least point us in the right direction).

Sometimes we have to delve into the unknown, go down the path that we've never been before to see if there is anything useful to us. We must stay open to what the unknown can provide, but we must also remain vigilant. We must realize that once we open ourselves up to possibilities, they can be good and bad. Just because something is an unknown event or path, doesn't mean it's the right thing to do just because it might hold some message for us. When these problems crop up, all we need to do is ask ourselves how we feel about it. Do we have any feelings of trepidation? Is there any reason that we think this is the right path, but are being lured away from the way we're really supposed to go? But there is also the positive side of the coin. All those things I just said could have a positive spin too, remember.

We just have to be open to the answers we receive when we ask questions, even if they're something we don't want to hear, but something we're supposed to hear.

ACTION MANIFESTO OF A MADMAN FOR GOOD

ENTRY#316

Being honest with ourselves is a great way to find out what we truly want to know. It sounds too easy right? I know it does. It's just something that we have to feel for ourselves. It's a way we can truly receive the information we're meant to receive and not what's meant for somebody else.

How often do we lie to ourselves on a daily basis? How many times a day to we tell ourselves we don't look right, we don't live right, or we don't act according to unwritten guidelines that some people blindly follow; this can go on and on and on till there is nothing left of our inner soul for us to move forward and find that positive.

I guess the main question that we have to ask ourselves is do we want to find something better? Are we satisfied with living hand to mouth and pay check to pay check while the people at the top are just getting richer off the bottom rung peoples' suffering and manipulation? Are we willing to just sit back and let the people at the top do whatever they want, while we sit here and wonder if they will ever let us get ahead.

Moving forward in an honest way starts with being honest about our situation, and if we've done anything to improve it.

ACTION MANIFESTO OF A MADMAN FOR GOOD

ENTRY#317

There doesn't appear to be anything wrong with the average person asking questions. When somebody is trying to gain information out of an authentic want to know the answer, will it come from a formulated thought that was focused group before they showed up, or will it spring up right in front of them?

The problem comes in when people ask questions for the pure purpose of stirring up trouble, not out of a want to actually know the answer. Or they are asking things that are in the form a question, but they are constructed in such a way that there could only be one answer given. And if the person listening happens to point out the wrongness in what the other is trying to say and attempts to answer the question truthfully, they're ridiculed to the point that they wonder why they were asked to appear in the first place.

We should never stop asking questions. But realize when we do, that the answer that comes out might not be the one we want to hear.

ACTION MANIFESTO OF A MADMAN FOR GOOD

ENTRY#318

Camaraderie amongst people and even amongst animals is how we survive when things are going bad, but also when things are going good. We are social creatures that are not meant to be put into our separate little boxes on our own separate little islands, never to know each other for fear of being contaminated by the other person's cooties.

We are not meant to be alone forever, even though a balance of some healthy alone time to gather our thoughts about what we should be doing is a good thing. Too often people are not giving themselves enough time to be able to reflect, sit back and enjoy the real beauty in the world?

On the same token, we should not spend all our time by ourselves, fiercely hold onto the beauty of the world so hard that we don't want to be around people, and only feel safe when we're completely alone and don't have to talk to anybody.

We are social creatures; we need to be around people. We also need to be alone. We must never forget to find our way to balance out the two.

ACTION MANIFESTO OF A MADMAN FOR GOOD

ENTRY#319

Putting good food in our bodies is a great way to keep our energy up and keep us focused. We could be the fiercest activist in the world, ready to fight for humanity in the same battles that people have been fighting in for centuries, but because of the foods we put in our body, we don't have the energy to create the corresponding action.

We know in our heart what we must do, but haven't reached the level of consciousness yet because we haven't learned that we need to fuel our body with not only love, information and the truth, but also quality food that gives us what we need to sustain us for the long haul.

Eating right can be hard when we're on a budget. We see the prices of organic foods and know we would eat them more if we had more money, but we just can't afford it.

We need to realize that all we can do is all we can do. As long as we're putting an honest effort forward to look for the right things, we will find what we need.

Sometimes we can't always find organic, but something that will suffice for the time being. Not only does this mean that we have to fight to put good food in our bodies (because of all the cheap junk crap food out there), but we have to tell the food industry that organic and natural foods will come down in price when they figure out it's cheaper for them to produce, once they start doing it in volume. We can do it if our intent is authentic.

ACTION MANIFESTO OF A MADMAN FOR GOOD

ENTRY#320

If fighting the food industry is a way to bring prices down on organic foods, how do we do that? Is fighting the right word to use considering that the workers are just people and would respond much better if they were talked to with respect just like we would? Are we bargaining with them? Do we have to show the big AG companies how they can make more money by making better food for them to start growing it? Are all the great advancements in human history (that will fix most of the problems we're going through) held back because we haven't been figured out how to make money off them yet; or maybe we have and it just isn't enough yet?

To save our planet with alternative energy on the scale that we need, we might need to appeal to the oil and gas companies. We basically have to appeal to the right people for the wrong reasons; this is the quicker way instead of completely changing their minds and fixing the entire corporate structure, which will come eventually. If the main focus of a business wasn't cranking out as much profit as it could and was for the betterment of humanity instead, the world would be a very different place. We would be a lot more open and giving society.

I know how we start the fight, but I don't know how we end it. Maybe we only have to know that we're headed in the right direction, and the rest will take care of itself.

As long our hearts, minds and intentions are in the right place, we know the first step, the rest are learned along the way.

ACTION MANIFESTO OF A MADMAN FOR GOOD

ENTRY#321

Sometimes we have to shed a few layers of protection we surround ourselves with to clear the way for something good, loving and for our highest good to come along. Politics are all mental. When authority figures lie to the people and their colleagues (and everybody they might come into contact with), it is just a ruse so they can execute whatever nefarious scheme they've cooked up.

Sometimes we have to shed parts of the wall we've built around ourselves so we can see the outside world, what its thinking and what it's trying to pull over on us. We might be surprised to know that that not all people are lying, trying to scam or bilk us, or are trying to be something other than what they say they are. This is when we need practice in not using a one size fits all approach. We need time to identify what is what by using honesty, because as lies opposite, it will always destroy it.

Sometimes we have to step out of ourselves to experience the true beauty and nature of society and the state of evolutionary change we currently find ourselves in. Stepping outside of ourselves can be scary, whether we have done it before or not. But, if we go into it with an open mind about receiving only lessons we're supposed to learn, then it might help answer a lot of questions.

ACTION MANIFESTO OF A MADMAN FOR GOOD

ENTRY#322

Do we spend enough time loving ourselves? Do we pour out all this love to other people and wonder why we might not feel like there is any left for us at the end of the day? Do we not know or not care to express love to others because that sounds like the kind of crap some weird person said back when we were in that weird place?

The more we travel forward in life we'll find that if we want to love others, we must love ourselves first. I'm not talking about being completely egotistical and thinking we are the only thing that matters, no. I'm talking about loving ourselves for who we are and everything we have. Once we feel the pure beauty emanating from ourselves, then we can spread it to others by just being around them and letting them know through words, actions or emotions that they too can feel the love that we feel. They will then have the chance to spread it to other people and so on and so on until the entire solar mega multi ultra-super-duper-multi-multi-multi verse is surrounded by white light so warm and loving, that we will wonder what took us so long.

All this starts with loving ourselves and not putting ourselves down. Can we do that for the betterment of all humanity?

ACTION MANIFESTO OF A MADMAN FOR GOOD

ENTRY#323

Have you ever wondered why ever increasingly insane attitudes and perceptions get us very angry, and distract us from what's really going on behind the scenes? Why do these attitudes take over all of our reasoning abilities and cause us to go into either a rage, or cause us to completely shut down and ignore anything coming from the top because we just assume its bullshit?

Maybe we just expect everything is bullshit, which causes us to not even try to make things better, because what's the point? Maybe we give up trying to improve ourselves or the world because we believe it's too far gone, so we enjoy the ride until the whole things blows up. Maybe purposeful ignorance is a coping mechanism so we don't have to deal with the real situation; and maybe this is one of the biggest reasons people at the top have all the power and influence they do. Maybe we need to take a look at ourselves before we take on the powers that be. Maybe we are the powers that be and we need to change ourselves.

Somebody said that we can't change everything but we can change how we react to it. Changing our reactions to the people at the top, and rationally thinking about what's going on, might be all we need to do.

ACTION MANIFESTO OF A MADMAN FOR GOOD

ENTRY#324

If we want to change our reactions to the bad situations around us, how do we do that? How do we know if our reactions will produce good outcomes or bad? If we start asking ourselves why we take certain actions or why we have certain thoughts, where will it lead us? Will it completely change our perceptions of the world, or will it just open us up so the real choices we have to make will be revealed to us?

We have the ability to change the way we see the world by asking ourselves why, why do we think the way we do? If the answer doesn't come right away, that's okay, life is a journey. As long as we pay attention to where we're headed and actually care about outcomes and consequences, we will end up where we're supposed to be.

We won't be able to find any solid answers to the big questions in life, but what we will find are clues that open up a whole new way of thinking. This will open our perceptions to the point where thinking outside of ourselves, and understanding what somebody else is going through will be commonplace and normal.

Reacting to people can be an interesting dilemma, do we get mad or look deeper?

We can get angry, it can make us feel better for a short period of time; but anger hides sadness and disappointment. If we look deeper, we will see that when attitudes get increasingly insane to the point where they make no sense and have absolutely no evidence to back them up, major world change is afoot.

ACTION MANIFESTO OF A MADMAN FOR GOOD

ENTRY#325

Ever heard somebody say that being open to life's possibilities will bring you all the things you ever dreamed of? You thought, what is this guy smoking? Ever heard somebody say that loving yourself and those around you will bring the right people into your life for the right reason and thought, how the hell does this person know that? Ever heard someone blurt out that the true nature of all the world religions, belief structures, human evolution and consciousness are based in love for all things and thought, WTF?

Hearing that somebody or something isn't the way we've always been told it is can really shake things up. Sometimes it can be like a two by four smacking us upside the head and knocking some sense into us. Sometimes we just aren't ready to hear it.

One of the most interesting parts of life's journey is when we find out stuff that we didn't know, or things we previously never thought possible. What we have to do is be open and realize that maybe what this person was smoking was the truth, and just wants to pass on the knowledge because that's what you do when you get it; you give it away, for free.

The purpose of learning to have love for all beings and all the cosmos is so we can spread it to as many people as we can. We learn and spread it to others so they can learn and spread it to more people, and so on and so on until we don't dream anymore about what a perfect world is like, because it will already be here.

ACTION MANIFESTO OF A MADMAN FOR GOOD

ENTRY#326

The idea of paying it forward has been carried out as long as people have walked the earth, and probably before that in the animal kingdom. Spreading love, help and caring because we got it when we needed it, is the way we become fulfilled.

I won't say we can ever be completely fulfilled and satisfied, "because life is a journey and not a destination" but we can get to a place where we feel we have a chance, like there is a crack in the wall that will burst through with the flood of our collective progress and evolution of consciousness (this will overpower any defense that has been set up).

Karma, paying it forward, taking care of our brothers and sisters are concepts within all our hearts and souls whether we realize or care about it or not. We can turn it off, we can keep it down, and we can even brainwash and torture it, making us think it never existed in the first place, but it will never go away. Love is here to stay; it will help push progress forward from thought to action for the benefit of all humanity.

We must always be vigilant with the knowledge we've been given, and realize that because everybody is at different stages of gaining that knowledge, we have to be patient.

We can collectively succeed when we realize everybody is at different levels and is just as confused as us. This is why we pay it forward, so we know we're putting out the love that we feel, even if we don't know why.

ACTION MANIFESTO OF A MADMAN FOR GOOD

ENTRY#327

I have no idea how to change the world exactly, but I know what I can do every day to make it a better place. Every time we go out of the house we should try to smile, and I'm not talking about that fake hi, how you doing smile that we would give even to the people we hate. I'm talking about that I love myself smile, that I love my station in life I love the entire multiverse and everything in it smile; and giving that to people we come into contact with. This isn't love that should be thought of as pushy, obsessive or weird; it should just be something that is completely normal.

There are definitely some of us out there that aren't used to somebody being nice to us, and filling us up with the love in their hearts. We might not know what to do when somebody looks us in the eye when they're talking to us, like it's some kind of threat that they're going to steal our food or something. Maybe the answer is as simple as the person that was talking wasn't centered in the truth, and they just spouted off as much crap as they could think of just to make themselves look good. Maybe the reason we aren't used to accepting love is that we don't know the intent of the person giving it. Maybe all we need to do to feel the full weight of the agape love is to just be.

Be the person that you always knew you were, but for whatever reason weren't willing or able to be even if you don't know how. Just making the effort means you are already halfway there.

ACTION MANIFESTO OF AMADMAN FOR GOOD

ENTRY#328

Making an effort to better the world can be a grueling experience that feels like it's ripping the very essence out of our soul; or it can be the most rewarding experience we've ever had depending on how we react in a given situation. It's our perception that guides our thoughts and intentions, which in turn gauges what our actions are going to be. The more we can think about our actions and what brings on those thoughts (so we know in the pit of our stomach we're doing the right thing), the more we will move forward with love.

I am not talking about over analyzing everything that goes on everywhere on a daily basis, that would drive us up the wall and we would never get anything done. We are a rational, thoughtful and perceptive people not only when dealing with others, but when we're by ourselves as well.

We must remember that life is what we make it. We can have a miserable time or a great time. It is our choice, it is our time, and it is up to us, now.

ACTION MANIFESTO OF A MADMAN FOR GOOD

ENTRY#329

Why don't we have health care in this country for everyone? I know politicians will say its socialism or it's communism, or it's a way the government can control everything in our lives; they might even say corporations and wealthy investors are what drive our economy, that they deserve as much profit as humanely possible so they provide the jobs that will grow the middle class. They might even be a Democrat and say it's the corporations that are keeping prices artificially high, and that when profit motive comes into the equation, it changes everything; they might say all that in public, but still take big money donations from the same people the other side does, which proves you might not be able to trust anybody. What do you do when there is nothing you can do, you do what you can.

We need to realize the time for real change is upon us, and we can either get on the train or get out of the way. Progress is coming whether we like it or not. We will try everything we can to bring everyone together. We will try to pour all the love of the cosmos into their hearts to change their souls, and start thinking in a different way. But, we will come to a point where we ask ourselves if we will keep going if nothing is happening.

Will we keep arguing and talking to a brick wall until we realize it isn't going to change no matter how hard we try? The question is, do we give up, or do we just come back another time when we're strong enough to show them the amount of love they need?

ACTION MANIFESTO OF A MADMAN FOR GOOD

ENTRY#330

Some of us need a lot more love than others to reach the point of being able to share it. Sometimes we put on a mask so we can hide behind the aura of being okay and cool, but really we're not. Sometimes all we need is for somebody to smile at us when we're not expecting them to; this might change our lives forever by helping us to start thinking in a different way.

Is there a way we can hook our love up to a receiver where we plug in once, and never have to think about it again believing we've done our part. Is there a magic wand we could wave so everything will just change already, because we're lazy and don't want to put in the effort, but we'll say we want to greatly improve the world for everybody and everything in it?

We must constantly give love so we can receive love and then we give it back again. This never ending cycle can be imprinted on our brains as something normal; even though it might not have happened in the past, it will now if we allow it to.

ACTION MANIFESTO OF A MADMAN FOR GOOD

ENTRY#331

Is there a way to squelch all worldly violence and hatred that's presently occurring in one fell swoop? Is there a way to just wave our hands and wipe the slate clean leaving only perfect people, where everything will be perfect and lovely and we won't have to think about anything anymore because everything will be perfect?

There is something to conspiracy theorists and others who think that one thing, one equation, one writing or one moment will change the world. They think the end of the world is fast approaching, fixing it is too hard or impossible, so they might as well scare people into fighting and killing each other so the end of the world comes sooner, proving themselves right.

We know what happens when we put effort towards survival. Do we also know what happens when we put effort towards what we have to do to evolve?

ACTION MANIFESTO OF A MADMAN FOR GOOD

ENTRY#332

Putting effort toward our goals and realizing everybody else is putting effort toward theirs can be daunting, but can be made a lot easier when we realize everybody might be out there trying to figure everything out, or nothing at all. Some people are out there to help us, and some might be out there to hurt us. As long as we stay open, we will receive information that is meant for us. If a person we come into contact with happens not to be for our highest good and/or out to hurt us, we will know right off and will be able to steer ourselves in the opposite direction.

Sometimes we are just in the wrong place at the wrong time, and there is nothing we can do to change that. But, since living our lives in a bubble isn't an option when we want to positively affect the world, we want to be remembered for more than picking our nose in third grade; we have to go out there and do something positive for the world, not just talk.

We must step outside of ourselves to find ourselves. Once we find ourselves, we can find others, and once we find others we can change the whole world together. We must make an effort to change the world, imagining is great, but it's only the first step in making it a reality.

ACTION MANIFESTO OF A MADMAN FOR GOOD

ENTRY#333

When we begin to see the wheels of progress turning, it can be a scary thing. Whether the change is internal or external the effect is the same. Will we fight against the tide until it bowls us over, or will we adapt to our new surroundings and take it from there?

Changing our sure footing out of the safe little rut we've built ourselves can be a lot of work. Deep down we might want to leap out of our cubbyhole and show the world we're ready to change the face of humanity, but don't for fear of being uncomfortable (throwing our special little corner of the world by the wayside). We must stand up to not only injustice and oppression, but also to ourselves when we know it's the right thing to do. Even though we might be uncomfortable and scared about what's coming next, we must move forward. Something within us tells us to carry on, that we will succeed if our hearts are in the right place.

Do we have the capability to make the change we know we can make if we allow ourselves to?

ACTION MANIFESTO OF A MADMAN FOR GOOD

ENTRY#334

When we have the backing to go after what we want, when we have the knowledge of what to expect around the corner, when we have love in our hearts for everyone and everything, we realize it's the root of what most people hold sacred. Will we take the necessary actions to spread what we know to the world? Will these thoughts we've had for as long as we can remember become reality?

Do we have enough power to surprise ourselves? Do we have enough love to wrap light around people that hate us? Do we have enough patience to know that we might not see the end result of our dreams in our lifetime? But, if we head in the right direction we will do our small part to keep the ball rolling towards collective and positive evolution.

ACTION MANIFESTO OF A MADMAN FOR GOOD

ENTRY#335

Why do we reach into a bag thinking the more we grab the more satisfied we will be, and won't have to reach into that bag ever again? Except what happens is, we reach our greasy fingers into that bag thinking it will be the final answer to what ails us. But is it the answer, do we leave all our eggs in one basket? Do we blindly follow whatever entity promises to do us no harm, even though we might get nothing more than lies and heartache wrapped up in authority? Do we try to get as much as we can as fast as we can before the boogie man comes to steal it away?

There has to be an answer to why we feel deprived when we don't have everything we want every second of the day. Now I know many of us might not have this problem, we might not feel everything will be taken away from us at any moment causing us to stock up for more than just the long winter. We might even love the job we're in and the family that we have around us, but do we ever stop wanting more?

There is a way to discover what makes us happy so we don't feel deprived all the time, just struggling for survival; it's called making the choice to be happy, and that's it.

ACTION MANIFESTO OF A MADMAN FOR GOOD

ENTRY#336

It's not possible for the world to immediately become conscious without any hesitation, where all of us realize that we're the same deep down and want all the same basic things just from different paths, or is there? Do good things happen all at once, or do they take time, or is that great things? Is it possible that the paths we're taking right now (right as we are reading these words), are the ones that affect the world and everything in it because we're conscious of it, or this is all a pipe dream?

There will be skeptics, there will be naysayers, there will even be bamboozlers wherever we go (which is why we must be courageously vigilant in locating what's for our highest good or not). We must be able to stand up for what we believe in, because if we don't, nobody else will. Well, somebody might stand up for us, but just the fact that we didn't stand up when we could have, will cause us to regret it for the rest of our life. We have to be strong and move forward. We must love the people that are around us and the ones that will serve a purpose in our lives that we haven't met yet. Maybe the answer is as simple as not only knowing what love for everything means, but also what it feels like when it motivates your soul.

ACTION MANIFESTO OF MADMAN FOR GOOD

ENTRY#337

There is nothing wrong with having fun and anybody that says so, is just saying that because they wish they were having fun instead of being grumpy (they just want everybody else to be miserable because that's how they feel, and if they can't be happy then nobody can). Picture this on a wider scale with one of us in a position of power and authority that has weapons and armies at our disposal; what happens when we want to blow off a little steam about how we woke up on the wrong side of the bed?

We must change the feelings in our hearts before they get out of control and there is nothing left but the memories about how we once loved. Do we just want to give up and say hey, the fights over and everything is too far gone to try to make the world happy, let alone ourselves?

There is a cure, it's called making the choice to be happy and moving forward towards fulfillment, or not. It's up to us to get where we want to go.

ACTION MANIFESTO OF A MADMAN FOR GOOD

ENTRY#338

Feeling happy, being a good person and doing the right thing isn't as hard as it seems. We just have to ask ourselves why we think that, and why now? Is there a reason that questions of moving forward, evolution and how nothing will be the same are coming up right now?

We are at a crossroads as a species and either can destroy ourselves, or build ourselves up in a way that raises our consciousness and speeds our comprehension of what's really important. We can have all the feelings in the world about something, but just because we think it's going to happen, doesn't mean it's guaranteed (nothing in life is no matter what anybody says). We have a choice, we have free will. We have the ability to know the difference between killing each other and helping each other live. We just have to remember to remember.

ACTION MANIFESTO OF A MADMAN FOR GOOD

ENTRY#339

The bed on the right side of the room is under investigation for armed robbery of a convenience store. Wait a minute, this isn't right, and we aren't even supposed to be here today. And besides, beds can't rob stores because they don't have legs. Beds can't carry guns because they don't have arms, and beds can't demand money because they don't have mouths. Politicians can't lie to the public unless we let them get away with it. But wait, there is a concern that any singular politician isn't the problem, it's the whole lot of them. So we get rid of all of them, and when they're all gone we elect new ones and put them in the same offices under the same rules; then they screw us over the same way politicians always have before, except this time we think it's getting better.

Then we remember that it isn't the politicians that are the problem, it's the system itself that's pulling the politicians strings, telling them what do, which way to vote and what bills to sign.

So the big question is, how do we change the system so "we don't get fooled" again as the Who would say? The answer is we stay open, honest and centered in the truth of what we're doing because it aligns us when we expect it to.

ACTION MANIFESTO OF MADMAN FOR GOOD

ENTRY#340

Bridging gaps and bringing people together is the key to so many problems. Yet sometimes we don't even try to make life better, we just stand in our ivory towers and wait for hellfire to rain down on us so we can take out our bows and arrows to fight off the hoard. Sometimes we're way out gunned and lose much of our blood and treasure. Sometimes we have a secret hidden (or not so hidden) weapon so we can destroy what's in our path without giving it a second thought. Sometimes we realize how completely ridiculous this all is, and just want to drop the gun issue and walk away; this fight can be solved with a conscious conversation and loving human energy flow.

We should try doing what we can, when we can. Trying to bring people together is never a bad thing. We must be vigilant in watching out for those of us who will stop at nothing to achieve more, and gain more of everything then everybody around them. These are the people that will be harder to reach. But we must never give up, we just need our own energy to be higher so we can handle it. This is where talking to not just the easiest people to convince comes in, but also the most perceptive and down to earth as well.

When we surround ourselves with positive, conscious and perceptive people, our energy starts to soar. Once this happens, we have a chance to take on those impossible to convince people and show them they can feel love too.

ACTION MANIFESTO OF A MADMAN FOR GOOD

ENTRY#341

Is the way a duck swims against the tide because they must find food to survive, the same way we must run against the wind of public perception so we can find out what really drives us?

Life sometimes is filled with hard decisions, a crossroads we all must face when we're given a choice to go one way or the other. We need to realize this is completely normal, everybody has the same growing pains of getting used to constant change as we do. When we're given a choice to not pay an unfair tax and the right to vote without reference to our standing in life or where we came from, it will be because we pushed the people in power and showed them there will be a day of reckoning if we lose our rights (it just might not be on their terms or conditions).

Love is the one constant that can sustain us through even the roughest hardships. It's the one thing that can always make us smile, always make us feel like we have a place on this planet and are here for a positive reason that we must discover. When we find what really drives us, the love in our heart will spread to everyone we touch. When we find love in our hearts, we discover that it's always been there, and has been what has driven us before. It was just waiting patiently for us to walk by and say, hello.

ACTION MANIFESTO OF A MADMAN FOR GOOD

ENTRY#342

Do we bring down governments to make ourselves happy, should we just take everybody out of office by force and install our own people? Do we become happy when every single little thing goes our way and we don't have to worry about any detail that could go wrong? Is the fact that we think for ourselves the way we should be moving forward to change people's minds and their hearts? I'm not talking about the fake Vietnam and Iraq and every other war you've ever heard of "winning hearts and minds". I'm talking about authentic action that comes from our soul so we can journey with people, instead of telling them what to do. If we just live out our lives telling other people what to do because we think we have all the knowledge one could need (and don't need to learn a single thing more), we will be empty and soul less and just as devoid of character and love as the government we mentioned wanting to bring down.

So do me a favor, don't guarantee violence and threaten your way to achievement if you flex your muscle just to intimidate the other guy. Just feel gratitude and love. Be thankful for what we have, because it will lead us to what's real.

ACTION MANIFESTO OF A MADMAN FOR GOOD

ENTRY#343

If we must come together to save humanity, can we save it in time to prevent the whole thing from going up in smoke? Is there a red line, a point of no return we could pass causing no amount of help, good will or consciousness to help us from going off a cliff? Is the whole idea that the world economy might collapse a mere pipe dream to manipulate the public into thinking they won't be safe, unless they buy a certain product or retain a certain company's services?

There was an old saying that said, "Beware of the wolf in sheep's clothing." Or you could take the line from I heard it through the grapevine by CCR, "believe half of what you see and none of what you hear." We have to experience life so we can make our own judgment on the scope of the problem; and even then we shouldn't take everything at face value when we do. We have to question things and take them with a grain of salt, but we must also love. It's the balance of the left and right brain that we must accomplish to evolve.

So once again we come to a choice. We can either buy into the line that "the world is already too far gone to do anything about it so why try", or we can get off our butts and do something that will change the face of humanity for the better.

Whether a red-line actually exists or is just a figment of our imagination, we will know we did our small part while we were here on this planet to make it better.

ACTION MANIFESTO OF A MADMAN FOR GOOD

ENTRY#344

If we're going to question whether it's the end of the world, not yet or even possible, we must start with what's real. Now while it's true that we create our own reality, when all these separate realities come into contact with one another they either bump each other like bumper cars or converge and meld into something completely new.

Is that what the world is, a big bumper car track where we bump into each other so we find the best spot to knock the other guy off their track before they knock us off?

Questioning is the first step in enlightenment. Knowing where to focus our questions so we can make the best use of our time is a little more difficult to carry out, but way worth it in the end. We can be discouraged when something doesn't happen as fast as we think it should. We must remember sometimes it takes time for things to develop.

We must stay ever vigilant that we aren't being sold a bill of goods, just because we are centered in the truth, doesn't mean everybody else is too. We must learn what to question and when to question, this is something that can't be taught, but can be guided.

How do we do that, we get out of our comfortable little rut and question why things are the way they are and what we can do to change them.

Because if we aren't here to help each other, then what are we here for, really?

ACTION MANIFESTO OF A MADMAN FOR GOOD

ENTRY#345

If we are here to help those of us who need help (including ourselves whether we want to admit or not), how do we know what direction to go first? Is there a blueprint so all of us can have a photo copy of exact directions on how to help others, and then ourselves? Or like the old saying, "we help each other when we help ourselves", are we required to help ourselves so we can feel love and the joy of fulfillment, and then show others the same thing?

Are we looking at it all wrong since there is no black and white answer to anything? Is it possible there are no directions anywhere on how to help people? We just need to keep our eyes and our hearts and minds open, and when we come upon someone or something that needs help, we should just help.

Sometimes it's difficult to figure out if things can be fixed or if we should take action (only we can decide when that point will be).

Outside influences will try to steer us in the direction they want to go, when we should be looking at our direction and the way we need to go.

We need to follow our hearts and let our soul guide the way. The more open and conscious we are to what's around us and in front of us, more of the actual future will be revealed, not a theory that has no basis in reality. We have to remember what is real and what is make believe.

ACTION MANIFESTO OF A MADMAN FOR GOOD

ENTRY#346

We must come together if we hope to move forward as a people. If this is truly the goal we want and really want to see peace in the world, we have to actually get up and take action. We have to show our neighbor that we love them and see them as a real person with real needs just like us that deserves the utmost respect. I realize that sometimes we might take actions that make us less respectable. We might rob a store, beat somebody up, destroy or damage something or any other number of destructive actions that would cause people to say we have no respect. So now the question comes up to me, how do we learn respect, and according to whose standards is that respect measured?

Trying to figure out what respect is and what a person should be feeling before we get involved in a certain situation is an impossible task, and anybody who says they can pull it off is probably pulling our leg. Sometimes we do so much prep work before the actual task comes up, that we feel we don't have to do anything more because we've prepared so much.

We procrastinate until the point that our opportunity has passed, and whatever we hoped to accomplish has also passed us by. This is the point we have to realize that there is no time like the present.

Procrastinating and over analyzing is a distraction that we place in front of ourselves to stop our progress. We do have the power to get out of our own way; all we have to do is flow like the river.

ACTION MANIFESTO OF A MADMAN FOR GOOD

ENTRY#347

There is something universal inside us that guides us in the right direction. Maybe we've just been asleep to it, been stuck in survival mode or haven't had the time to think about it. Maybe we just haven't thought it was a big deal because we could always muscle through any problem we faced if we were focused and ready for anything.

What is it inside of us that make us not want to admit when we're wrong? What's in the deepest darkest pit of our stomach that says "hey, you're fucking up and must change your course?" Whether this change involves shifting our way of thinking or our way of interacting in the world with the people around us, the effect is still the same. Sometimes we know about the change we need to make but have ignored it, this is when we have to ask ourselves if we have purposely done anything to prevent this connection from happening.

Are we the ones causing all the heartache that prevents us from moving forward? Are we the cause of our problems even if there are vast outside resources trying to fight back and push us down? Sometimes we might not be able to change these violent or dominant forces trying to push us into their camp, we can only change the way we react to them.

They might be violent, mean or rude to us, but if we show them love and an open mind, then maybe they will see how they're screwing themselves up by messing with us.

We're all connected, when we hurt somebody else we're just hurting parts of ourselves. The sooner we find this out and see how much this idea permeates many of society's problems, we will see how the solutions to major historical problems aren't as impossible as they seem. Sometimes we must stand in our own way, but sometimes we must let ourselves go free. It is up to us, it is our choice.

ACTION MANIFESTO OF A MADMAN FOR GOOD

ENTRY#348

If unions and civil rights organizations are out there fighting for the rights of a group of people, are they fighting for us all if one person changes their perception of a problem? Does that idea spread to everybody and help them realize that not only is it our hopes and dreams that are connected, but so is our oppression. Whether we are the ones who are oppressed or are the ones doing the oppressing (or maybe we are the ones who are witnessing it but aren't doing anything to stop it), what we do affects everybody else.

There are certain things we must do to get along in society today. We need a place to live, food to eat, clothing to wear, maybe some love in our life, which usually requires a job to support it all, or none of it might be achieved. Or is this what the people at the top want us to think. Do we need a job to support our self? I guess that depends on what defines a job. It seems as long as we have some sort of income stream, the money changers don't care where it comes from as long as it's coming and there is no bad press about it (cause that way they won't look bad or like they're involved with anything nefarious).

We are one people, one community, one planet. What we do ripples out like a stone thrown in a lake. We have the ability to positively affect the world by spreading authentic love and happiness to everybody. Will we work towards it, or will we expect it to be handed to us? We have that choice and it is up to us.

ACTION MANIFESTO OF A MADMAN FOR GOOD

ENTRY#349

Ever heard the old saying there is a time for work and a time for play? What if we're trying to get some work done when friends and family call to hangout or help them with something, and we question if we want to because we really want to get done what we have set out to do. Whether we are working on something for our job, hobby, or because it's something that we hope will eventually make us a living, we must ask ourselves what are our priorities at any given time.

We must ask ourselves, if we set a goal to finish doing a project, is that goal realistic, is it within our reasonable bounds that we can finish? If it is, can we ignore or just put off friends and family that might need our help or our moral support because they're going through a tough time?

If it isn't realistic, are we just thinking up things that are taking up all of our time so we don't have to think about anything that has to do with the project we're working on, even though we probably won't finish it in the first place? See anything wrong with this picture, anything we could change in our thinking processes?

When we feel that a friend needs a shoulder to cry on or even a friendly ear they can talk to or even vent to, we must be there no matter what. We find that by being open and ready to receive information we're meant to receive, we will hear our friends when they need us. The idea is to know when to put off our own needs for somebody else's. Does this come when we realize that we need help one day, so we help others out in favor of building up our own karma? Or do we help out friends because it is the right thing to do?

We must help people whenever it feels like the right thing to do. We must bring them up when they're feeling down, and let them know that there are people out there that care for them. Why you might ask do we do this, why do we do we care for this person? Because we know that if we were in the same position as them, we would want them to do the same for us. If friends aren't there to help each other out, what's the purpose of anything?

We must see that social interaction is what makes us thrive as a species. Loving each other and making sure everybody realizes that fact is how we evolve.

ACTION MANIFESTO OF AN MADMAN FOR GOOD

ENTRY#350

If we react to one another in either a positive or negative way, is there a method of interacting that will skew it more one way than the other? Is there a way to gauge whether what we are doing will steer collective consciousness and evolution in the right direction, or heaven forbid in the wrong direction? Can we as a people begin to see how what we do ripples out, sending out good vibes instead of bad ones meant to do us harm?

I know I ask a lot of questions in these books. I seem to not know what I mean to say all the time. Well, I think I might be in the middle of my own process as well. I am discovering every minute of every day and in every page of this book I write that the world is a little less like expected, and a little more unknown. I want to find the answers so I can figure out not only how I can be the best person I can be, but also a better world citizen. What can I do to make my time on this short earth the most rewarding and fun time I could possibly have? How can I leave a positive mark? What can I do when I know what to do, but I don't know what to do?

I love that I don't know anything but staying open when I'm exploring the unknown. I do my best to stay centered in the truth of what I am doing so I know I'm moving forward.

The only way to gauge whether something is going good or bad, positive or negative, good or evil, yin or yang, is through love. Are we expecting love to come to us when we don't do anything for it, does it come naturally, or do we have to put it out there to get it back?

The best thing we can do for ourselves and the planet is just to put love out there, even if we don't know why or where, we should just do it. Even if things don't end up the way we planned, at least we will know that we did our part to put love out to the world. The fact that we might skew something negative or positive won't even be a question, because we will know that it came from a place of love. And when we do that, we can never go wrong.

ACTION MANIFESTO OF A MADMAN FOR GOOD

ENTRY#351

We must start from a place of love and peace of mind, if we want to fix the world's problems. We must start from a place of compassion, if we want to bring warring peoples together. We must start from a place of tolerance, if we want to have a chance at the peace we dream about. We must start from a place of humility, if we hope to have a chance to compromise.

There are some universal truths that have always held true. We have laws of gravity, the laws of attraction, the theory of relativity (which is way over my head), and we also have the law of love. There are many others that are among us every day, but I'm not going to list them all here, sometimes we learn more things in life when we have to discover them ourselves. Now these laws aren't written down in any traditional sense, they don't have a book of codes and a whole court system structured to carry out the letter of the law; people live, breathe, try to be happy and do the best they can (or at least that is how it's supposed to work).

There is inequality, racism, sexism, all matters of persecution and ethnic and personal retribution, and yet what do all these ideas have in common with each other? How do they seem to be part of the same idea, and what are they all devoid of?

The answer is love; the answer to most questions is love. We have to see how love can permeate actions we take or are thinking of taking, and how things might turn out differently if love was at the forefront of our thinking all the time. We must start from a base that we know will work. When some of us were (and continue to be) skeptical of the Beatles when they said "all you need is love", maybe we don't know what love actually means.

Maybe we think we must do and achieve everything we're trying to accomplish in life before we should feel and deserve love and respect. Maybe we are thinking about it all backwards. Maybe we need to start with love and then start working our way out, instead of always working our way back to it.

If the shortest distance between two points is a straight line, its gets even shorter when we realize we have the opportunity to start from a place that brings the end closer to us.

ACTION MANIFESTO OF A MADMAN FOR GOOD

ENTRY#352

Have you ever rolled out of bed and not known how to start the day? Have you ever rubbed the sleep from your eyes while your mind looks for something to focus on, so you can begin the ball rolling for the day that's right in front of you? Ever felt the different effects of thinking bad thoughts and then starting your morning routine and getting out the door, as opposed to starting off with good and loving thoughts and seeing where that takes you?

It makes a huge difference to our human psyche when we treat life with the love and positivity it deserves. We can build up the hopes and dreams of ourselves and those around us if, we pay attention to the simple rule of love and understanding. Within this rule is where "seeing somebody as yourself" comes from. If we feel positive, spread love and give to everybody we come into contact with, it becomes very contagious. I know I've talked about this endlessly throughout this book, and some people might even say that it sounds like I'm repeating myself, but that's the point. I feel sometimes we've strayed so far as a people from what is real, that it's going to take a gargantuan effort by all of us to pull off saving the world.

We need to repeat things to ourselves a lot sometimes before they sink in. If negative thinking has been ingrained in us over the years it could take a while to change it.

For some of us thinking positive is always the way it's been, and we might say, "people that think negative have always been the problem and we shouldn't try to help them, we should ridicule them for not making as much progress as we think they should have." This is when we need to be patient and realize everybody is on their own journey in their own time, and deserve just as much love and respect as we do.

If we're used to being loved and see it as an everyday thing, we must have patience with the other side, and help them to feel what love and understanding is really all about (not just intellectually know of their concepts).

So when we wake up in the morning and attempt to get our thought process firing we must remember, we can spread to others whatever we're feeling whether it is negative or positive. But we must ask how we would like to feel. Do we want to feel love and respect, and have the ability and opportunity to positively change the world? Everybody else just might want the same thing.

ACTION MANIFESTO OF A MADMAN FOR GOOD

ENTRY#353

If we know we can unite and work together, what's the turning point, what will make it happen? What will be the one event or person that will help us see only our commonalities and not our differences? For instance, if health care costs keep rising and not offered to all the people that need it (other than the emergency room where it's vastly more expensive), it bleeds back into the original problem of not affording it. Given all this, how can we make the prices come down?

Some people say the way to make healthcare cheaper, is to take all the burdensome regulations off of the manufacturing of meds, so companies can make more supply and bring more to the people; the problem with this is there's no proof it's ever worked or will ever work. It also might cause prices to rise even more if all these private companies that make these drugs think of profit first, and safety second; this is a problem when you're taking care of people, you need to care for them first, especially when dealing with a medicines quality.

Which brings me to the other side of the coin that says the government should put more regulations into manufacturing of drugs, their procedures and equipment, because it will be safer to the consumer; plus the price would come down because this way of thinking would make the government want to pay for the healthcare through Medicare for all or some other sort of socialized medicine because it's cheaper. This can be a problem because some people might fall through the cracks.

This basically proves that no side of the coin has the monopoly on a solution. Nobody has the magic wand that will get all of us covered while keeping the price down. We need to come together and find a solution that we all agree on, but when we negotiate we have to be honest with ourselves and what our goals are. Do we want everybody to have quality affordable health care? Do we want them to be healthy and productive members of society?

If we really want to come together over this, we must not only negotiate in good faith, but also realize that the other side might have some better solutions than we do, so we should listen for that nugget of truth. We never know where an inspiration might come from. We just have to ask ourselves what we truly want, and then go after it and make it happen.

ACTION MANIFESTO OF A MADMAN FOR GOOD

ENTRY#354

Compromise, negotiating, coming together and being human to each other can be a hard thing when we're at each other's throats all the time. Has the world of politics always gridlocked when two sides can't agree and/or can't come together? Have we always been so stubborn that we can't come together over what we know we already agree on because politics and self-aggrandized reputation fogs the truth, preventing us from doing what we can because we're worried what somebody else will say?

Politicians have always been funded by people they later gave favors to, which might include being their friend when laws are proposed that affect them; many times have they let the fog of politics block the truth, preventing the real issues from being negotiated because they weren't willing to settle for anything less than 100% of what they want. This is something that has always permeated our system, but only lately has gotten so bad; we have to ask ourselves why this is? Why does it seem to be so much worse now?

To get the real answers to the real questions that we have in our hearts (but are afraid of going after because of what other people might say), we have to ask ourselves what we actually want. Not what our friend, family or biggest funder wants, but what we want.

We must also ask ourselves what the people that we disagree with want and how they feel about it. If they're similar, it might be the answer we're looking for.

ACTION MANIFESTO OF A MADMAN FOR GOOD

ENTRY#355

If we do some introspection and find that what we're looking for is very similar to what other people are looking for, is it the first step in coming together? Is discovering that the person we've been fighting for days, months or even centuries has way more in common with us than we previously thought (because the differences are why we've been fighting in the first place) the first step in realizing the world might not be like what we thought, and we might not have it all figured out?

When we have our turning point, when we have that light bulb go off in our heads, we must pay attention. Something inside us might tell us that the person we've been fighting for centuries over land, power and influence, are probably looking for the same thing as us. This might tell us that we've been going about the fighting all wrong. Maybe the fighting was wrong in the first place; because we don't want to give anything up just like the other side doesn't want to give up anything, we will be constantly butting heads, which won't get us anywhere.

Once we come down into the valley and off our high horse, we will see that no matter how much we say the reason we're fighting is the other persons fault, it's really us and how we reacted to the original issue that started the fighting in the first place.

If we react differently, they might react differently, and the problem might be solved. We will never know unless we try.

ACTION MANIFESTO OF A MADMAN FOR GOOD

ENTRY#356

The truth is what the truth is. We arrive at the table of public opinion with much life experience we may or may not have had, and put together what's true for us. This can come to be our truth, just like everybody else is figuring out their truth. When everybody is out looking for their own respective truths, we must realize all of us are going to come to the table with our own truths, which by definition will be different than others.

When we come to the table with a truth that is constantly changing and evolving whether we want it to or not, we must realize that questioning somebody else's truth isn't the way to bring them to our side (in fact it might be the fastest way to turn them away). We must respect somebodies truth, and get them to ponder why they feel the way they do about something. For instance, instead of asking somebody if they believe in the free market, ask them how they believe the free market will make the changes we all need to see. On the other side, if we ask somebody why they believe in socialism, they might be instantly defensive. What if we asked them how they believe socialism would help make the changes we all need to see. It's the same question on both sides, but put in a way that doesn't threaten or question our beliefs, it's just gets us to elaborate.

Elaborating and explaining ourselves can bring our thoughts and actions more into focus, or it might show us where we need to change. To receive the information we need to receive and come to a place we need to get to, we must realize we all have our own truths that deserve to be respected, which can help us grow when we try to help others grow as well.

ACTION MANIFESTO OF A MADMAN FOR GOOD

ENTRY#357

What's the matter with Kansas, what's the matter with San Francisco, what's the matter with Washington D.C.? What's the matter with questioning something we think isn't right? Is there a way we can do it where the other party doesn't feel threatened and actually wants to negotiate because we're interested in what they have to say? Does this cause us to be interested in what they have to say because we don't see them as the enemies anymore, but a wellspring of learning about the other side?

When we ask what is the matter or what is the problem with the other side, we must first start with ourselves. If we perceive a problem with a certain group or a certain area that we assume holds a certain kind of people, we must ask ourselves what we think the problem is. We must find the exact reason we think the way we do, and what spurns our thought process, blocking out other thoughts that upset what we're trying to tell ourselves. Once we find the reason, we might find that what we've been trying to decipher about the other side isn't so much about actions, but how we react to them. How we question and how we build up our defenses can help or hinder us. But that's the point, it's up to us.

We can choose to bring us all together or tear us all apart. But before we ask what is wrong with everybody else, we must first ask ourselves what is the matter with us.

ACTION MANIFESTO OF A MADMAN FOR GOOD

ENTRY#358

Any law that blocks access to information, entertainment content, or us going through certain doors at the building where we are watching a speaker, is something that must be questioned to see if it's justified. The tricky part is when we begin to analyze, we might find that there are two sides to everything we come up with.

We might want to allow public access to all information about government and its operation through all of its departments and subsidiaries. If we feel it's the public's right to know everything their government is up to, we won't feel like we're living in a state of secrecy that tells us we will receive all of life's luxuries, as long as we don't question where it came from. At the same time we might want to prevent access to some information for security purposes, like what our troops are doing and where they are. This is when definitions have to be respected, by both sides, which means that the definition can't shift just because somebody felt like it.

Even if we block access to copyrighted content or a certain door when a meeting is going on, we will always have our different opinions on both sides of the issue. As long as the definitions don't shift, we will have an honest debate.

Are we pursuing an honest debate because we feel it's the only way we can solve our problems? That question includes being honest and truthful, and not changing according to the whims of ourselves or the public.

ACTION MANIFESTO OF A MADMAN FOR GOOD

ENTRY#359

Just like muscles can atrophy from inactivity, so can the mind. If it's been awhile since we've thought critically, our mind can atrophy to the point where we don't question; we just take everything as it is, and don't seek to improve anything cause that's just how things are. We must exercise our muscles so we can be an active member of society, or better yet, an active member of our life. If we exercise our minds and our bodies, we will find we have abilities we might have forgotten about.

Being active and eating right is what keeps us healthy and gives us the best opportunity to live into old age and still be productive. Being active and critically thinking about the world around us, is how we keep our mind healthy so that we are still with it and still know and care about what's going on. When our mind goes, our body might start to fail us too.

The mind and body are connected; one can't work without the other. Therefore it's very important we realize they work hand in hand (when we benefit one, we benefit the other). Once we not only know about this connection, but feel it as well, we will see everything that's in front of us. To see we need to feel, and to feel we need to see. Once we see this interconnection, we will see how everything else is interconnected as well.

ACTION MANIFESTO OF A MADMAN FOR GOOD

ENTRY#360

What can we learn from the predator prey relationship? First the predator stalks its prey by picking out the weakest of the bunch because they're the easiest catch and don't fight back much. The prey in this scenario may run and put up a fight, but it's the predator that ends up winning. This equation usually ends with the predator full and happy, and the prey lifeless and dead.

Why do I bring this up? Look at the governmental and economic system we have in this country, isn't it exactly the same? When the government decides it's going to cut taxes and cut spending because we are in yet another budget crisis, do they take from the weakest first? Do they do this because it's the easiest thing for them to devour, so they decide to pounce? Does government realize they might be able to handle one prey, but when there are millions and billions of prey, their numbers are much too small which will cause them to run for the hills?

Do they know their power is based on an illusion, and instilling fear that the whole thing is going to blow up if they don't get their way? Are we going to be the predators or the prey? Maybe a better question is, are we going to love or are we going to hate?

Are we going to realize that to breakout of this endless predator prey cycle that we can't be out to dominate others, and shouldn't put up with being dominated ourselves? We are here to live together.

ACTION MANIFESTO OF A MADMAN FOR GOOD

ENTRY#361

The fact that we're here to figure out how to live together so we can consciously evolve as a species is a given. The fact that we all know this, I would argue is also a given. What isn't a given is why we know it, and still don't do anything to change it. Sometimes we think living together is too hard and we should just try it tomorrow, or its not comfortable and we just don't say anything; or we say we don't care but in fact we care the most, we just have a lot of excuses. Sometimes we wallow in what's comfortable and think that if it's at least comfortable and all our needs are met in the physical realm, we won't need anything more.

We have to tread through what's uncomfortable to get to what's great, which might tell us what our dreams are all about. Maybe the problem is that we all know there is a problem and know what to do to solve it, but we don't say anything because we will be thought of as weird, a troublemaker or somebody who always complains.

All we need to motivate ourselves is to believe in ourselves. We will succeed if we just stay focused on what's important in life, and are open and ready for any opportunities that come along the way.

We must come to a point where we all realize that we are the answer to our problems; we just might have to get of our own way.

ACTION MANIFESTO OF A MADMAN FOR GOOD

ENTRY#362

Believing in ourselves and giving ourselves credit for what we've accomplished will replenish our soul, and make us want to strive for more. Not that getting accolades from friends, family or just some guy on the street for our accomplishments isn't a good thing, because it is. All I'm saying is we're the ones that we've been looking for. Giving ourselves credit for things we've done even though we might not have finished them is important. Being thankful that we have the opportunity to make a difference or even simply just having a job so we can survive, is the way we gain confidence, determination and the love that will help propel us forward.

I know it sounds like I might be getting ahead of myself, and I am counting way too many of my chickens before they hatch. But that's just it, we must look forward for what we need and how we want the world to be, and then go after it with confidence and love because we know it's already ours, we just need to retrieve it.

We must know some of the things that are in store for us, so we have some idea of what we're chasing. The thing is that we're way better off if we learn the whole thing as we journey along our path, instead of learning it all beforehand; because even though we might have learned about looking ahead from a book or from endlessly thinking about it, it doesn't mean we know how it feels or what its possibilities really are.

Life can't be taught, it can only be learned through experience. We must realize that learning how everything works beforehand and then entering the fray, means we will have to work backwards. We will want to be way at the end without putting the work in because we see where things can head. We feel that just because we learned everything about it, that that we've earned the right to just spring ahead and collect our prize.

We must learn as we go. We must build ourselves up and not tear ourselves down, before we try to build up others. We might find that we're helped much more when the person trying to help is consciously doing so out of the goodness of their heart and a want to do-good. We must treat ourselves like we would like to be treated, and then we will know how to treat others. Is the answer that simple? We will never know if we don't try.

ACTION MANIFESTO OF A MADMAN FOR GOOD

ENTRY#363

How do we break free from oppression? How do we bust off the locks that are holding us back, preventing us from moving about in freedom and good will? Is there a chance we will meet a special locksmith randomly as we're walking down the road, and they will have just the key to bust us out from the chains that hold us from our true potential? Or do we have to look at all the possibilities of life, and look at why the locks and blocks are there in the first place, who put them there, and what they're made of?

There are endless answers to the question of how to break away from oppression, as there are endless answers to what makes up that oppression, its history and goals. We have to get at the fact that we're all in this together. The more we see each other as the same deep down, and hold each other responsible for our transgressions, the less we will be held back.

The point is to look inward and realize that we might be the one locking and blocking ourselves. In which case, we must ask ourselves why. And if we search and search and can't find an answer, we simply ask why not?

ACTION MANIFESTO OF A MADMAN FOR GOOD

ENTRY#364

If we're assessing life's possibilities and telling ourselves we can't achieve something, or a task is too hard and we think we can't possibly move forward, we must ask ourselves why we think this, and why we're thinking it now. If we can't figure it out, we ask ourselves, why not. If we don't figure it out on the second go around, we ask why not again.

We must keep asking ourselves why not until the thing we're trying to accomplish becomes so blatantly obvious and seemingly impossible not to get, we move forward with a confidence that can better all of humanity.

When we were in school we were told to ask questions when we needed help with a certain problem or if we didn't know something. Since questioning is a skill that doesn't go away with age (it only gets more detailed and honed in), we must start asking ourselves questions instead of just the outside world. We need to fully find out what makes us tick like we might have never done before.

Once we have a better understanding of ourselves and of introspection, we will see what works and what doesn't, which in turn will make us want to get rid of the bad stuff and keep the good stuff.

When we get our full and uncensored analysis of ourselves, we will see that everybody out there is doing the same. One might ask why, I would ask, why not?

ACTION MANIFESTO OF A MADMAN FOR GOOD

ENTRY#365

If governments and militaries control the country, who controls the people? If corporations and Wall Street control the money and the economy, who controls the people? If the even shadier folks in the shadows (of which we never know their names) control all of these entities as their overlord of sorts, I ask again, who controls the people?

The reason there is no answer to these questions is because nobody controls the people but themselves. If people choose to be corrupted, or they fall into a cycle of survival (unable to think of anything else), then they're being controlled by other people, not faceless entities. Everything has a face, it just might not come forth in the place we expect, or in the form we expect.

ACTION MANIFESTO OF A MADMAN FOR GOOD

ENTRY#366

If our end goal of thinking outside the box and asking questions is to come together around what we already know we agree on so we can work on the deeper questions, and have a better chance at answering them, what's next? Should we automatically expect that the deeper answers will show up, because we have already come together so we don't have to put any more work in? Should we just blindly follow whatever sounds right, or should we put thought into things we do?

We can't just sit idly by and wait for everything we want to just fall in our laps. At the same token we also can't put so much effort into actions that we're forcing them to happen, when maybe they weren't meant to happen. Where is the balance? Where is the even ground between being open and ready to receive, and forcing things to happen that we really want?

I don't have a solid answer to what everybody should do all the time, all I can do is provide groundwork, a foundation to work from. We must ask ourselves what is causing our mistakes to happen? What can we do to better our lives and humanity, what is the answer to the question we all ask which is, when are things going to get better? Well I have one simple answer for that one; things get better when we get better.

ACTION MANIFESTO OF A MADMAN FOR GOOD

ENTRY#367

The old saying that the world doesn't revolve around us is only about half true, or should I say that it's one of those things that is true and not true at the same time. The world doesn't revolve around us, it keeps spinning around no matter what happens, because it has been there long before us and will be here long after us. The world might revolve around us however when we see that the root of most of the world's problems can be traced to what we tell ourselves, and how our feelings and thoughts can be magnified out to the whole world. We all seem to be the center of all our own little universes.

One more example of balance in action is, once we start paying attention to the signs and beauty that's all around us, we will start to see examples of it wherever we go. This will only reinforce the idea that we can accomplish our dreams when we finally get out of our own way and are going after the right things.

So whether the world revolves around us or not (or both at the same time) doesn't matter in the end. What matters is how we treat others, and how good thoughts and energy magnify out even more then the bad.

ACTION MANIFESTO OF A MADMAN FOR GOOD

ENTRY#368

So what exactly can be fixed in this world and what can't? Is there ever a way to get corruption out of politics, or do we have to put up with a rigged game forever? Is there a way we can feed the hungry folks on the street, or are they going to be there begging forever? Is there a way that we can feel empty and alone when we're surrounded by people and completely at home and loved?

The answer to these questions and so many others lies within us. We have the answers that we've been looking for, and we are the people we've been looking for. We get corruption out of politics by not being corrupt in our own lives. We feed people on the street so they aren't hungry, and help them build themselves up so they aren't begging forever, thus ending homelessness by ending what creates it in the first place. We tell ourselves all sorts of things to get worked up; but if we slow down and ask what we really think and actually hear the answer, then we will end up where we're comfortable, wherever that might be.

So what can be fixed, the answer is us. Once we fix us, everything else will fall into place.

ACTION MANIFESTO OF A MADMAN FOR GOOD

ENTRY#369

Certain expectations are bred us into at an early age, what we are supposed to be, what makes a real man or a real woman, along with a real patriot or citizen. These precursors to our enlightenment can be hard to get passed especially when it's the only thing we've ever heard, and don't know anything else. We must ask ourselves what purpose they served, when they came about and what purpose they serve now. If the answer is precursors serve no purpose, then that's an easy one, we just get rid of them and are done with it. If there is a purpose, then we have to look deeper.

Looking deeper is hard especially if we've never done it before or think it's stupid; the funny thing though is if we can come up with a reason why it is stupid, then we're looking deeply into it, which completely disproves our original point.

We are just people looking to get along in this world filled with so much darkness. Once we realize that we're all in this together, all this light shows up as if it has been there the whole time; maybe?

ACTION MANIFESTO OF A MADMAN FOR GOOD

ENTRY#370

Are we in a race against time, or are in a race against ourselves? Does time even exist to time this race, or are we really going to spit out any thought that comes into our head? Are we going to move forward and fix what we need to fix, or we going to slow down and eat shit when the going gets tough?

Sometimes the questions we ask can be uncomfortable; this is when we must weigh the pros, cons, consequences and repercussions of asking in the first place. And just like anything, if the good outweighs the bad, then we should go for it. Life is all about moderation, fun and responsibility to the earth, our species and to us.

Whatever we discover our mission in life is, we can rest assured that as long as we're searching, the path we're supposed to take will appear.

ACTION MANIFESTO OF A MADMAN FOR GOOD

ENTRY#371

As the answer to most questions is love in some form, the answer to most problems is hate in some form. Is this true or is it just an illusion? Is this just a question meant to distract us, while the paycheck writers change everything by working behind the scenes to make us want to buy their products and vote for their officials? Is there a problem with brainwashing people into killing or oppressing others as they sleep with their families, is it something that can be fixed with love and understanding by preventing these things from ever happening in the first place? Are all these questions getting old?

We must always stay vigilant that we don't get told love is hate and hate is love, because then we won't know what to believe. What we must do is love and not hate. Is that so hard, does it sound like just a hippy concept from all those dreadlocked people that don't know anything about anything? Or is loving and not hating such a universal idea that even though some of us have been asleep to it for so long, we can easily pick It up again whenever we choose. Love will bring us everything we need when we use it, and we can spring forward from it. We use it as the fuel in our tanks to better the world.

ACTION MANIFESTO OF A MADMAN FOR GOOD

ENTRY#372

Going out and talking to people can be such a rewarding experience, especially when we realize that every moment and every interaction is a chance to make the world just a little bit better. Try it. Walk out the door and smile at somebody. Strike up a conscious and tolerant conversation about the state of the world. Experience a new culture or event never experienced before. We can go out and take on the day, and surprise ourselves by striving farther than we ever thought possible.

Being out in the thick of it, experiencing life by tasting it, is what sticks to our soul and builds up our psyche infinitely more than learning it out of a book. Books are a starting off point, a place that gets us interested and sparks our brain and inquisitiveness into action, but it's only the first step; the next step is to use that knowledge and apply it.

Using the things we learn to better the planet and humanity is why we learn them in the first place. The time may come when we learn something bad, and we tell ourselves there is no way it could ever be used to better the planet. This is when we must look a little deeper and ask if we should simply tell people the information, or just stop the stuff from happening in the first place. And if hearing bad information makes us want to leap into action and right the wrongs that we've heard about, then a bad thing can serve a good purpose.

We find out the good and bad meaning of everything when we truly step outside of ourselves and experience the realness of life. We find what we're looking for when we slow down and look in the mirror.

ACTION MANIFESTO OF A MADMAN FOR GOOD

ENTRY#373

The idea of sharing our thoughts, opinions and feelings is universal. We are a social species; we always feel the need to be close to people. Now there are specific times when we like to be isolated, this is when we have time to slow down and step outside of ourselves to get a bird's eye view. Alone time can be useful when trying to figure out things that we need to get past, lessons we need to learn, what actually happened during our day, or the way our life is leading. We need to balance this alone time however with a healthy dose of being around good people, beings that brings us up and not tear us down, people we can really just let our hair down around.

Finding the balance between being around people and being alone can be difficult, but it becomes much easier when we look inside and ask ourselves how we really feel. Chances are the real answers will be revealed to us if we pay attention. You can call it being conscious, being open, being present, seeing or just paying attention, but the fact remains we're better off not getting hung up on words and phrases because they can end up holding us back themselves.

ACTION MANIFESTO OF A MADMAN FOR GOOD

ENTRY#374

Does a cloud represent that a dark and powerful storm is about to blow in releasing enormous of destruction and doom, or is it simply that all the bad storms and darkness are being cleared out to make way for warmth, light and love? Or is it somewhere in-between?

If life is what we make it, we have the ultimate choice. We can choose to see all the bad in the world; we can choose to see that it's just getting so much worse that destruction, famine and genocide happen so frequently and powerfully that there's nothing we can do to stop it, so why even try. We are better off not thinking about it, and just enjoy the world until it blows up in our face.

We can also choose to see all the beauty in the world, and see that more and more is being revealed to us if we are open to it. We can make use of all the beauty we see by spreading it to others, because we've finally arrived at a time when the vast majority of us will finally be reached. We will be able to come together more than ever before.

We can also choose to be somewhere in the middle, trying to figure out what we want to do with our time. We take everything in, keeping the good and leaving the bad.

We use what we learn to make up our own way of thinking and go forward the best way we know how. We are all at different stages and might need more or less time, but the point is if we make the effort, we can come together.

ACTION MANIFESTO OF A MADMAN FOR GOOD

ENTRY#375

What doors are open to us in life, and which ones aren't? What opportunities are obvious, shouting at us in the face to come and take advantage of all the things they can give? What opportunities are more secret and hidden, taking much more effort to find them, but sometimes paying off much more in the end?

Figuring out what opportunities are really there, and which ones aren't can take much practice and vigilance to gain a firm hold of our surroundings. Sometimes though, it's simply relaxing and just being open to what's around us that makes the answer appear. Have we ever been stressed out about a certain situation and felt there is no way we could ever find our way through it, that there is no way we could make it easier or go away, so we just give up? But it's not this act of giving up that serves the real purpose, it's the act of letting go of our all our insecurities and blocks that we've put in place to stop ourselves from moving forward.

We will find out more often than not, that when we slow down and not let fatalistic and negative thoughts cloud our brain, we can relax enough to allow the real thoughts in. It's almost as if we allow it by clearing the way, or opening the door.

Will we open the door when we find it, will we slow down enough to realize that we might have been staring at it the whole time?

ACTION MANIFESTO OF A MADMAN FOR GOOD

ENTRY#376

Doors, windows even portals to a certain extent provide a great example of how all the choices we have in life are just waiting for us to accept, or ignore them. There are lots of things that bombard us on a daily basis meant to distract us and get in our way, some of them are self-inflicted and some aren't.

The best thing we can do for ourselves is to be open to all these chances and choices that seem to be floating around, and check them out. What do we have to lose if we try to fix something that everybody agrees is a problem, but think can never be fixed, or just don't do anything about because we're stuck in a survival, self-preservation or egoistic mood?

Life is all a big series of what will we do on a daily basis. Will we go this way or will we go that way? Will we stand up for what we believe in or not? Will we be the example of what we want to see in the world because we realize that real change starts with us and spreads out? Will we constantly and endlessly be searching for that answer, that one thing that will change everything?

Will we see that the more of us that try to fix problems on a personal level first, before we go out and try to fix things for other people, is much more effective because we can authentically lead by example? We can be our best friend or our worst enemy, it is our choice.

ACTION MANIFESTO OF A MADMAN FOR GOOD

ENTRY#377

So if life comes down to opportunities and choices, is there a way we can ensure that these will always be obvious to us? Is there a method for guaranteeing that what we're supposed to do to change the world and how we're supposed to do it will be broadcast on a big movie screen with flashing lights?

Is it pure luck that we stumble upon these opportunities and chances, and don't have any say in them because they happen completely at random? Or is the fact that these opportunities and choices come up all the time, make us the ones that decide to see them or not by the way we block or allow them into our mind?

There doesn't seem to be a blue print, an end all be-all way for every one of us to ensure that all things that are supposed to happen will, and all things that aren't supposed to happen wont. The best thing we can do for ourselves first and then everything and everybody else after, is to not block ourselves, not stop what is supposed to happen by being negative and making ourselves think something can never occur.

Once we unblock ourselves, the clouds will clear away and the real truth will be revealed to us. We have a choice, do we take advantage of what's in front of us, or do we let it go and wait for the next thing?

The answer will be revealed to us when we see what we hear and hear what we say. Being as authentic a person as possible will only lead us to where we're supposed to go.

ACTION MANIFESTO OF A MADMAN FOR GOOD

ENTRY#378

If stepping outside of ourselves and thinking about our situation is the best way to see what's in front of us, then how does that apply to the historical, governmental and political problems that we face every day? How does clearing our own roadblocks correspond to changing the Electoral College so the popular vote has the final say on who wins an election? How does figuring out what prevents us from moving forward correlate to allowing rights for all people regardless of their gender, religion, nationality, creed, sexual orientation or class? How exactly does working on our own issues help fix the world?

Think about it, if everybody fixed what was wrong with them or at least made an honest effort at it, how would the world look and what problems might be prevented? Is it possible that if everybody concentrated on making themselves better people, that everybody they came into contact would just feed off their energy because they've figured out what is universally important? Are asking questions the way to start on our path of finding an answer?

ACTION MANIFESTO OF A MADMAN FOR GOOD

ENTRY#379

Allowing ourselves to heal, not trying to rush the normal process our bodies have to go through to recoup losses, must be taken care of if we hope to accomplish what we dream. We must see that when we've been blindsided by hate or intense pain we suffered at the hands of something or somebody, we can't truly move forward until we realize that our life is what we make it, and nobody else.

We must be conscious and pay attention to what's going on within us, so we know what's going on around us, not the other way around. We must realize that the outside will give us clues about how we are and what we're about, but it's the inside that reveals what is supposed to be seen. It is us that have the power and the choice to make a difference. It's up to us to get off our butts and do what we all know needs to be done to fix the problems that need to be fixed. If any of us still don't think it's possible to do anything about the major problems, ask this, if we're not part of the solution are we part of the problem? Or even a better way to put it, are we blocking the positive evolution of our species by not allowing ourselves to evolve?

We must find out where we're at to figure out where we're going.

ACTION MANIFESTO OF A MADMAN FOR GOOD

ENTRY#380

Once we realize the problems we face, (the destruction, the persecution, the downright ugliness), along with all the great things that surround us like love, peace and harmony, what's next? What do we do to start this train moving? Once we've come together around what we already know we agree on, how do we use that to change political, social and governmental environments?

The only way to find out what we're supposed to do is to stay open, and move towards what we feel is right. We might not know where life is going to end up, we might not even know if the finished product will be in the same form as when we started, but that's not the point; the fact that we accomplished our dreams and did what we felt was right for the sake of humanity is the point.

We must delve into the unknown to truly figure out ourselves and the rest of the universe. We must keep moving towards light and warm energy even though we might know where it's going to lead, but that's the point, we don't know. When we find we still have the ability to surprise ourselves, we know it's the first day of the rest of our lives.

ACTION MANIFESTO OF A MADMAN FOR GOOD

ENTRY#381

Will reading spurn thoughts that will lead us to usurp and overthrow all the old ways of thinking that have come so close to causing our destruction? Will watching movies or TV make something click in our brains and make us see all the bullshit and ugliness we've created? Will we see that we've created all the bad ideas and people that are destroying us, and we're the only ones that can come to the rescue? Can any kind of media give us the message that will be our light bulb moment, or will it be somebody walking down the street, who or what will it be? We might say to ourselves, "I'm so anxious and I want to know now, I don't want to wait anymore because I shouldn't have to. I don't want to put in the effort to fix the things that I can fix. I just want them to magically appear all better."

Certain messages, slogans and signs come in all forms and bombard us all the time whether we see them on a billboard, or within our soul. What we're supposed to do will be revealed to us when we pay attention. Since there is no solid answer of what we should all do, how can we ever expect to relate to somebody that is doing something completely different than us?

When everything is stripped down to its root, and we see that everybody is going after the same basic thing and coming from the same basic place, we can use it as a starting off place. If we allow ourselves to start from where we are the same, the possibilities are endless.

ACTION MANIFESTO OF A MADMAN FOR GOOD

ENTRY#382

There is a reason that we get defensive when we feel threatened. There is a reason we get all up in arms when something happens that we don't like, whether we react by using actions, words or even by staying silent. There is a reason we all feel we deserve an honest shot at making a good life for ourselves and the people we care about. There is a reason that we rush to someone's aid when we see them lying on the street being walked over when they're at their most vulnerable. There is a reason that even though we might be scared shitless of the unknown, we move forward anyway because we know in our heart that it's the right thing to do.

Ever heard the saying, "there is a reason for everything", and thought "yeah, but we couldn't possibly know what it is?" Ever thought there could be a universal feeling and thought that drives us in the right direction even though we might not have the end result figured out? We do have the power to be the change we want to see.

So what is this reason I keep talking about (using repetition again in my book which I have been very fond of throughout my manifesto)?

The reason is love. It's what drives us, or it's what tears us apart. It is up to us.

ACTION MANIFESTO OF A MADMAN FOR GOOD

ENTRY#383

Are there ways we can wake up to what's around us, and finally see what's in front of us because we are ready to admit what's inside of us? Is knowledge of wrongdoings and evil behaviors enough to put a stop to them? Do we actually have to share this knowledge with the right people for something to happen, or can we just keep it bottled up and simmering until one day it boils over and we just go nuts? Is there a balance between being the only soul knowing the information, and actually sharing the information with the right people, or all people depending on what it is?

We can all come together, we can all relate and unite, we can also all see what we're supposed to if we pay attention and feel the weight of the situation we're in. We will do what needs to be done in the name of saving the planet, and taking down the dams that we've erected directly in the path of our own progress and evolution. It is possible, we can do it. We are our biggest cheerleader, so go team go, go team go, go team go. Go out there and do what needs to be done.

ACTION MANIFESTO OF A MADMAN FOR GOOD

ENTRY#384

When we ask questions aimed at getting under the surface of our ingrained thinking, we must realize it will ruffle some feathers and rattle some cages. When we get knocked out of our comfortable surroundings, all sorts of things appear that might not have been apparent to us before; there could be massive unemployment, there could be a housing crisis, the poor could keep getting poorer while the rich keep getting richer. There could be all sorts of things that appear when we pull the veil from our eyes that has kept us warm and cozy in our own ignorance for so long.

When we pull this veil away, we must realize that all sorts of bad things can happen, or should I say that all sorts of bad things will become obvious and apparently spring out from nowhere. When this flood of information comes in, depending on how we look at it can gauge how our mood identifies what's in front of us. If we look at everything darkly, the unknown will appear scary and out to do us harm; we might yearn for the time when we were comfortable and everything was simple because we didn't have to think about anything, people thought it for us. But, if we look at everything with light and openness, we will find that everything coming at us now is there for our betterment if we allow it to be.

We might think a piece of information is bad because it tells of a factory with slave labor, which makes us sad to think about where a product comes from. Or we could think it's good because this story of oppression and gross negligence gives us the opportunity to end suffering of a group of people that could have continued on with no end had somebody not spoken up

All of life's problems depend on how we look at them; they have two sides, and therefore we have two choices. Guess what they are?

ACTION MANIFESTO OF A MADMAN FOR GOOD

ENTRY#385

I'm not making some kind of grand statement that will save all of humanity, one speech that will bring everything together under one idea and one unity, nor do I want everything to be the same. Sometimes I think there are forces fighting for their survival by having us fight amongst each other for our survival; other times I think it's more than that. What if the problem of the rich moving higher and the poor moving lower has something to do with what happened in our childhood? Maybe we're constantly trying to prove ourselves so we don't feel bullied because some rich kid bullied us when we were young. Maybe our parents told us that sometimes to climb the ladder we had to step on some people on the way to the top, and crack a few eggs to make an omelet.

However we were raised, (whatever we experienced that brought us to this current point in our life) we must see how it's affected our thinking, for the bad and the good. We can get past what's holding back our progress if we have the strength and courage to not block our path in the first place. Sometimes the most courageous thing we could ever do is to get out of our own way.

ACTION MANIFESTO OF A MADMAN FOR GOOD

ENTRY#386

We must move forward even when there doesn't seem to be an apparent way. What do we do when it looks like there's no way out? Do we carve our own path when the cards are stacked against us? The paycheck writers and Wall Street barons have said they control everything so we better not mess with them; they have done this by building into the system an internal debate that has no point. It keeps us bickering about and to each other, so distracted that we can't see past what's right in front of our face; which we would be able to see if we weren't blinded by our own thoughts.

There is no way government, corporate and Wall Street powers will just relinquish their stranglehold without a fight. But we must ask ourselves if this stranglehold is real, do they really control everything? Or does it just seem like they control everything because sometimes we play right into their hands?

We can't be scared of what we don't know and what we've never seen before, it could be the jumpstart to our evolution; we will inherit it if we're ready. We can do this.

ACTION MANIFESTO OF A MADMAN FOR GOOD

ENTRY#387

Critical mass is what we need to save the world and show the people at the top their control is an illusion. If we amassed enough people, (I mean a crowd that would make occupy look tiny by covering city blocks and many neighborhoods) the level of anger and frustration that's been brewing in the heart of this country would explode and shoot forward with progress like we've never seen before.

Getting a crowd together to do certain things could be great. Some people might blow up buildings, some might kill people, but that isn't who we are. We must not fight this fight with hate and destruction in our minds, that's what the people want who keep us fighting each other so we don't fight them. If we stoop to their level, we will never evolve or fully see our true potential.

All we need to do is have a crowd gather and then just be. We can be the world we want, we just have to create it (Like occupy but on a massive scale). It would be nice to gather a few hundred thousand people, but if we gathered 10 million, there is nothing any military, police, or other government structure could do, short of executing its own citizens (which has happened to many other countries on their own soil, just not ours).

We must stand up for what we believe in, we do have the power. In huge numbers, we can achieve everything we've collectively dreamed about. We can make it a reality.

ACTION MANIFESTO OF A MADMAN FOR GOOD

ENTRY#388

When things change and evolve, when situations change without warning and cause an up swell of positive or negative energy in our soul, we have choices. We can join either side of a conflict; we can join the side that has dropped many bad things on our heads over the years. Or, we can join the side that is fighting to end that power and make it go back to wherever it came from. What if there is a third way, what if the answers weren't so cut and dry? What if the whole idea of their being two sides is the main problem? What if the whole idea that we're split into two different camps is the ultimate tie that binds, making it impossible to move forward because we're so locked in?

Situations, events, people and places always have evolved and always will whether we want them to or not. What if the act of bring us all together simply means bringing us all together. It's easy to talk to somebody when they agree with us and say yes to just about everything we say, it's much harder when somebody doesn't agree with us and might not even like us.

We must not see ourselves as on two totally different sides, but both parts of the balance that we must achieve on the same side.

ACTION MANIFESTO OF A MADMAN FOR GOOD

ENTRY#389

Is the glass half full or half empty? Is there any real point to that question, or is it just a way to categorize our way of thinking so we don't have to be taken seriously? Why is it necessary to categorize us at all into groups, forcing us into pre-ordained ideas of what we should be and how we should act? Is this necessary, or do some of us just think it's necessary because it's all we've ever been taught?

Personally, I think the glass is half full, and I would never demean somebody for thinking it's half empty. Some people are positive thinkers and some are more negative thinkers, or as they might like to say "realistic thinkers". But again, it only matters how we look at it. If we look at the negative reality in front of us, we might get a really dark picture that would love to pull us down, by discounting the positive. But, if we look at the positive reality of what's in front of us, we might get a happy and loving image, which will lift our energy the more we feel it.

I am a half full person, although I am not advocating for either full or empty. Why we think the way we do and what makes us better off in the end will come with hard credible evidence to prove our point. This is something we must find ourselves because it can never be given to us, it can only be discovered.

ACTION MANIFESTO OF A MADMAN FOR GOOD

ENTRY#390

There might be trepidation when we start seeing the light at the end of the tunnel, when we finally allow ourselves to see the end of a long task. There might be fear over what happens in the years ahead as collective social uplift, humanity and accountability permeate back into our culture after being lost for so long. There might even be grief over what and who we've lost so far; the losses might be even heavier in the future when we really get under the skin of the powers that be.

Love, happiness, and smiles have always been more powerful than darkness; we must seize the opportunity in our time, right now. Critics might say "every generation has said that it's their time and their turn to make their mark on history". What these critics don't get is all of us have thought this before, if only but in the moment. By thinking this is our time now, we do what we feel we can by moving forward and leaving a positive mark on ourselves and those around us.

Simply put, we do what we can; it's really all we can do. If you take some of the greatest people in history, all they were ever able to do was take it just that next step. The best thing we can do for ourselves and humanity is to take it that next step, but upward, outward and forward.

We will never know if we can achieve the light at the end of the tunnel if we don't try. But if we do put in effort, we will see that not only that we can achieve it, but that we already have.

ACTION MANIFESTO OF A MADMAN FOR GOOD

ENTRY#391

If we love the people around us with all our heart and soul, and use that to bring all the best to humanity (which brings us to that next step of evolution), are there always going to be distractors coming through our field of vision helping us to prove our point?

If we stay open to what we're supposed to hear, we will receive what we're meant to receive. If we enter the fray of changing the world and bring up positivity meant to get rid of the world's negativity, we will probably be met with resistance. This negativity might be seemingly impossible to overcome with anything less than bigger armies and bigger guns than they have. If we stay open to the world, we will see that those resisting are the ones that need fixing, and the fact they're so mad and angry means they're really thinking about what we're doing.

Getting the other side to think is the first step, getting the other side to change their direction is another. If we realize in the end we're all meant to come together anyways, things will become much more apparent. The question might come up, well what about people who absolute refuse to breech their opponent's side, but won't give up the fight?

Is this part of the balance that we've built, does it play into our plan? We will know if we look inward and always question what we think, so we can understand what other people think.

ACTION MANIFESTO OF A MADMAN FOR GOOD

ENTRY#392

We must come to terms with where we're at so we can figure out where we're going and what path we're supposed to take. Are we at a place where we can grow as people and start thinking out of the box because there is this whole other world out there we might not have thought of before? Are we collectively at a place where we can use out of the box thinking to see the distractions placed in front of us, keeping us from uniting around what we already know we agree on? Are we at a place where we can come together, and use that unification to fix injustices we've had since the beginning of human kind?

I realize I ask a lot in these books, I say a lot of things that might be far from the norm. I have been through trying to balance questioning with bringing people together many times before, that sometimes I play down its importance in favor of some pressing need in my daily routine.

I just want to do my part in bringing us forward. I know these are just some books and one guy's way to say what he wants to say, but I really feel we can accomplish everything I've said in this book, and the two previous. I haven't uttered a word I didn't think was possible, or didn't have some anchor in the truth.

I feel right now is humanity's best chance to do what has always been known would fix what we already agree are problems. It's finally the breaking point when the dam is going to break, and a deluge of progress is going to come through. Are we going to block it, or are we going to roll with it?

ACTION MANIFESTO OF A MADMAN FOR GOOD

ENTRY#393

Are we going to have enough energy to make it across the finish line of justice, or are we going to fall asleep at the wheel because we can't keep up? Is there a finish line at all, or is it just an illusion that keeps us motivated and moving toward what we all know we can achieve?

Will we or wont we, it seems like that question has been asked since the beginning of time. How are things going to happen, how are they going to work out, what are the consequences? We might want to know everything about everything before we even make the attempt to change the world, until then will we just study up and prepare? We want to know if we're looking ahead at trouble, if it will be clear skies or if we might have to change our course midstream. We want to be prepared, but we don't want to be uncomfortable. We want to love, but not too much. We want change but only if somebody else makes it.

We must never use laziness as an excuse, and we must always do what we can when we can. We must realize however that sometimes a situation might not be ideal, but it requires our attention. We must not be scared of the unknown, we must embrace it for the lessons we might learn. We don't want to shut down before the party begins.

ACTION MANIFESTO OF A MADMAN FOR GOOD

ENTRY#394

The reason we start unions is the same reason we start organizations dedicated to fighting for rights of a certain group of people. The reason we can't put up with all the crap being thrown at us is the paycheck writers and the barons at the top don't know when to stop. As producers of the crap, the top dogs will keep throwing their weight around as long as they keep making money and/or until we get buried.

We must always ask ourselves why. Why do we take on huge corporations that do us wrong? Why do we protest laws that we feel are unjust? We do we petition the government for a redress of our grievances? Why do we want to be free?

Being free is a human emotion. From Africa to Asia to the Middle East, the Americas and all points in between, freedom is wanted by those that do not have it, and frowned upon by those who know it will bring them less money and influence. We must see how all peoples want to be free, and how all of us can do something to make it happen.

How do we find that one thing we can do that will bring everybody together? Stay open, it will come.

ACTION MANIFESTO OF A MADMAN FOR GOOD

ENTRY#395

Is falling asleep at the wheel of your car and careening off a cliff that ends in a fiery explosion, the same as the government asleep at the wheel of the economy and careening it off a cliff until everything explodes but them? How is the government able to protect themselves when they go flying off a cliff of their own doing and survive not only intact, but still way better off than most of us? How are they able to do that? If we go flying off a cliff, don't we explode on impact like something out of a movie?

What has falling asleep done to our economy, our government, our humanity and our psyche? Have we relinquished power so that we could have the illusion of security and peace of mind? Or are we just taking a break so we have plenty of energy stored for when the real battle or confrontation begins?

We must find what we've lost and what we can gain from the struggles we've endured in this country, as well as what people have gone through around the world. When we look a little closer, we will find that we have all gone through the same sort of stuff, just in different ways and with the same idea behind them. This commonality is the tie that will bind us together so we can move forward without getting nearly as tired.

So the next time we feel like falling asleep at the wheel, just remember we can always tap our buddy on the shoulder to take over for a little while. We are truly in this together, when we realize we are **ALL** in this together.

ACTION MANIFESTO OF A MADMAN FOR GOOD

ENTRY#396

People will always be linked by virtue of being human, but what if events happen that are so severe that it questions our humanity so forcefully it smacks us in the face. What are we doing to better each other, are we building each other up, or are we tearing each other down? Are we directly being part of the problem by pushing others out for believing differently than us, even though we might not want to admit it? Admitting guilt is one of the biggest problems we have in society; and when people in a higher class of life admit guilt, they aren't always held as accountable as somebody in a lower class in life.

Some of us are higher class and some of us are lower class, and many of us are in the middle. The point is we are all in there somewhere, struggling for all the same things. Remember kindergarten? Remember the idea that everybody should be punished equally if they do something wrong. Think about rich kids being treated differently than poor kids, is this any different than treating white kids different than black kids? Is pitting one group of people against the other the only way for the people at the top to maintain their illusionary iron grip on forward mobility?

We must come to a point where we're comfortable in our travels and that even though we might not be as far along in life as others, we're happy because we see where we fit in to the bigger scheme of things. Once we realize everybody else is also trying to find their place, than we can really make some change to move in the right direction.

ACTION MANIFESTO OF A MADMAN FOR GOOD

ENTRY#397

There is a time and a place for everything, just like there is a common emotion within that will sustain us, whether we want to admit it or not. All things and all people can make a difference if they really want to, but they can never do it if they only say they want to, but don't mean it. Nobody can ever get the job done if they go at it half-ass. Would the Great Wall of China have lasted this long if they had done a half-ass job? Would the time and effort put in be wasted if all the bricks tumbled down, crushing their hopes of something that would really protect them?

We must figure out what links us all, and what we have gone through in different times and on different paths. Love is a blinding force that can make everything brighter, beautiful and not so gloomy. We must learn to give to all people at all times. This is not something that is learned overnight, but it must be learned.

If there is a time and a place for love, it is now and forever.

ACTION MANIFESTO OF A MADMAN FOR GOOD

ENTRY#398

Do we ever feel like we've done everything, seen everything and sure as hell have heard everything, then something comes along that blows all our original thinking out of the water? Is there ever a time in our lives where we come to a crossroads when a decision has to be made that will affect the rest of our lives and everybody around us?

We might feel a bit overwhelmed when it comes to the choices, decisions and consequences behind our decisions that we have to make all the time. It might seem like there is a wall growing that prevents us from moving forward, because we tell ourselves we don't have time to progress with all the crap we got to do.

This is when we should ask ourselves, are we purposely sabotaging ourselves so we never progress? Is this because it might entail going into the scary unknown that we don't have full control over? Are we at the point where we have enough energy to combat the onslaught of distracting forces that attempt to take our minds off what's really important? Even though it can be tough sometimes, finding time for reflection is crucial.

If we don't ever think about what's going on in front of us and what it means, then we will be forever wondering why everything happens. Do we want to float around forever, or do we want to be grounded?

ACTION MANIFESTO OF A MADMAN FOR GOOD

ENTRY#399

Are we running against the wind when we fake like we care, just so we can go onto the next thing and the next thing and the next thing? Is it like salmon swimming upstream to spawn only to find a dam blocking their way? Or is it like people waiting all day in line for concert tickets?

The powers that are in control have been in control for a very long time. The reason they hold the positions they do is because everybody just assumes that it's always going to be that way. We lie, politicians lie, everybody lies and that's the way it's always been and that's the way it will always be. Who said that things will never change? Was it some wise professor that studied the idea for a very long time before coming up with an educated solution? Was it the people at the top controlling things, holding their people down by putting out messages that things will never change? They've even twisted the message to say that what they're doing is new, when it's really something old, just in new packaging. This is done so they look good with the public, who thinks they've turned over a new leaf, and everything is all good.

What the public fails to realize is that people always have an agenda, good or bad, and that is why it's always good to ask why certain actions were taken. Why did this action happen, who stood to gain, and what are the repercussions?

Finding out why we're running against the wind is the first step in finding out how to run around it or through it. An opening is there, we just have to stay vigilant and poised to see it.

ACTION MANIFESTO OF A MADMAN FOR GOOD

ENTRY#400

The people at the top are getting scared of the power that we're building; they know their iron grip is slipping and have to drum up extra support for the distraction factory that has doubled its production as of late. The top dogs get scared of what the millions and millions of us at the bottom might do if we ever got together and decided to force them to act in a better way. We could shut this country down by all walking out on the job all at once, like a school walk out, but nationwide. Imagine if it only happened for one day, what if a hundred million people walked out of their homes, jobs and schools and banded together to demand their grievances be righted, and their injustices be made right? This is what the top is afraid of.

Before we get too confident that the top is in their last throws, we must ask ourselves if we're trying to distract ourselves again from the real task at hand. Are we, just by way of being overconfident, giving up ground and giving back into those distracting forces that kept us down in the first place.

We have a hard enough time lifting ourselves up and trying to lift up others, that if we try to put ourselves down as well as others, we won't have nearly enough energy to do what we need to do.

We must ask ourselves, what is the better use of our time, moving forward with what's new, or not moving at all, and sometimes inching backwards with what's old? We have a choice, it is up to us.

ACTION MANIFESTO OF A MADMAN FOR GOOD

ENTRY#401

What do we do when we feel so strongly in our heart that we want to better society that we get anxious and bored with our surroundings? Is there a way to end all this anxiety without relying on pharmaceuticals? Do we have the ability to heal ourselves so we can see that even though it might look like somebody else is holding us back, it is always us, and has always been us that has the final say? The government creates rules that might make it next to impossible for the public to see real changes on a national level; but that doesn't mean we can't make the change within ourselves and have it permeate all the way through 1600 Pennsylvania Avenue.

We can remember to see the beauty all around us and how the world looks when we strip all the triviality away; it's a place that's made up of a bunch of humanoid based life forms all running around struggling to make life a little less difficult and a little more fun. Some of us might have forgotten what's really important in life, but as always, it's still there, waiting for us to dust it off.

We can make the change we seek, we are the people that we've been looking for, we just have to slow down and realize it.

ACTION MANIFESTO OF A MADMAN FOR GOOD

ENTRY#402

Figuring what we want to do isn't easy. Figuring out what other people should do is impossible, but if we find what binds us together, we will find the universal truth that everybody from all classes and races have been waiting for.

Do we fight or do we compromise? Do we stand up for what we believe in or do we negotiate to end the bloodshed? Do we admit that many of the distractions in front of us are self-inflicted, and in the same fashion they are self-healing as well? Is there a way for somebody somewhere to wave a magic wand to make all this stuff come true tomorrow, or do we actually have to put the time in and work hard to make it a reality?

I thought I might have all the answers when I wrote this book, that this installment of the madman series would be the end all be all that would catapult me into an action oriented status in one fell swoop; kind of like Clark Kent changing into Superman in a phone booth in an instant. It's turning out to be something even more real than that for me. It's a way for me to put out thoughts and feelings I feel most would help impact the world, and help us all to get moving in a positive direction.

I've always felt very passionate about making change, that I really felt like I wanted to do something or create something that made a difference. By the third book, I thought I would be changed, would not need to put in anymore work, and could just bask in the sun of progress and the feeling that I've done something. What I have come to realize, is that this is not the end, this is just the beginning, and this is the door that opens me up to the rest of the world.

ACTION MANIFESTO OF A MADMAN FOR GOOD

ENTRY#403

There is something very familiar about working together to achieve a goal or get past an obstacle, like something bred into us at an early age so we could carry it with us throughout our lives. I guess the question now is, how are we doing with that? With the everyday problems that we see, are we making a conscious effort to bridge the gap preventing us from coming together around what we already know we agree on? Are we working with one another and not against one another? Are we able to slow down long enough to receive the information there to help us get passed whatever we're struggling with?

We must attempt to go towards what we want and need because if we don't, who will? The difficult part is separating what we want from what we need, so we can get our priorities straight. We can do it; we do have the power to organize our lives, to put the importance of the wellbeing of our souls first (for the very reason that we share it with others). Once this effort happens, it gets the ball rolling, which reveals that self-preservation is universal. Collective preservation will appear through our everyday actions just to prove a point. How do we get the ball rolling?

We just have to slow down, pay attention and be mindful.

ACTION MANIFESTO OF A MADMAN FOR GOOD

ENTRY#404

"Pay attention to what's around you" sounds like something our mothers told us when we were growing up so we wouldn't bump into things or walk out into traffic. It doesn't make the saying any less true when we're constantly bombarded with crap that flows at us with no apparent meaning whatsoever. But, if we look a little closer we will see that our first glance isn't always true. Maybe the crazy story on the news wasn't what actually happened, and maybe the official government press release is just a glaze to pacify the public. So if this is true, (and I would argue it is) how do we know what to fight against when the airwaves are flooded with all sorts of mixed messages? When do we stand up and say hey wait a minute, this sounds like bullshit to me? When do we sit down and listen because we can tell that it's some important stuff?

We can tell the difference between things when we pay attention. We can tell that an apple and orange are different because we look at them. To know if it is edible fruit that we can consume, we have to peel back the skin to see what the flesh looks like underneath. So is the same with news and the information projected at us, we must peel back the skin to see the truth underneath.

ACTION MANIFESTO OF A MADMAN FOR GOOD

ENTRY#405

So we peel back the skin to see the truth of what's actually going on around us, then what? We have all this raw information, what do we do with it? What does it mean and how can we possibly use it to prove or disprove something?

First, it always helps when we pay attention. If we don't pay attention we might miss something very important and useful, clogging ourselves with all sorts of information not useful at all. But, if we pay attention we will pick through the mass of misinformation to find the shiny little nuggets of truth.

I must admit, I question myself sometimes, I mean who doesn't. I try to tell myself that everything will get better if I try to make it so. And then sometimes when things don't work out because of my fault or otherwise, I get down on myself and start thinking I've been wasting my time with all this mumbo jumbo.

The thing that keeps propelling me forward is staying open to what's around me, and seeing all the beauty I have a chance to see on a daily basis. Then I remember something an old journalism teacher taught me, which is following the money, and you will find the truth. If we follow the money trail, ask questions and pull back curtains, we must be ready for what we find. Once we pull back that curtain, it can never be covered again. The misinformation that was hidden will be out in the open for the world to see. We must prepare for what the people will do who hid it in the first place. We must realize they might be upset we're airing something they don't want aired, and must be ready to counter their anger with love so they fall out of their familiar cycle.

When we pull back the skin, we never know what we will find, but we do know that it will be authentic. It will be the fruit as it truly is. What we do once we know, is up to us.

ACTION MANIFESTO OF A MADMAN FOR GOOD

ENTRY#406

If we follow the money, we will be shown the way. If we are shown the way, we must be prepared to take that first step or the truth boat will pass us by, forever drowning us in a sea of ignorance. Who is funding the messages and who is funding the government, corporations, NGOs and all other outside groups? We must know why things are being said, and what their motivations are.

Do we want to know the truth? Do we want to be free of the chains that have been locked by ourselves? We must remember that no matter what ugliness we see or what we uncover, we control what we do. We have the choice to make a difference or not. We are the ones that decide what's important and how to live our lives. We are the ones that create governments in the first place; politicians come from us because they are us. Once we change the way we look at each other, it will change the type of politicians we elect. Once we change the type of politicians we elect, we will change the system. And once we change the system, we will be well on our way. Do I know what happens in the end, of course not. I am no sage or swami, I am just a regular guy that wants to show everybody in the world that we'll be all right with one another, when we truly "hear" and "see" one another.

Once we truly see one another, sometimes we see a money trail leading back to some really bad shit. We must have the courage to see what this really means and ask ourselves if we contributed to it, and/or how can we help. We are here to help each other out, right? Is there anything more human than lending a helping hand? We just have to make sure that the person we're helping isn't hurting us in return.

ACTION MANIFESTO OF A MADMAN FOR GOOD

ENTRY#407

How far is that rainbow, and why do we have to go after it? Who says that we have to go anywhere, because this looks like as good a place as any? What is this force I've heard some people talk about that helps you out along the way? Some people call it Spirit, God or Allah, some a tree or an animal, some just an energy force. Some even don't feel anything at all or choose not to feel it because of personal beliefs or experiences.

We have come a long way in our evolution; from the times of king and empires, to slavery, through freedom, independence and civil rights we have persevered for what was right. If we haven't fought, it was because we were too scared of what might happen if we did. We didn't know what to expect, or were told something that later turned out to be completely false.

We know all the time and effort that we've put in to doing the right thing will pay off, or do we? Whether we answer yes or no to that question will prove how far along we are on our own journey.

Do we go over the rainbow to get what we want, does the pot of gold really exist, I don't know.

What I do know is that if we love more than we hate, think more than we block out and hear more than we listen, we will be positively surprised with what we find. How we interpret it is up to us.

ACTION MANIFESTO OF A MADMAN FOR GOOD

ENTRY#408

I think therefore I am, or I think and therefore I can see. And once I can see, what can I do? I am a person that decided to think, or not to think. I am the one who made decisions based on what I put together in my head, or by sitting on the couch and doing nothing.

Gandhi once said, "live like you were going to die tomorrow, and dream as if you were to live forever." I would take it a step further; I would say living means doing. Doing means changing, and changing means upsetting things and then setting them right. Do we want to set things right, or do we want to just leave them as they are?

I could harp all day about how Wall Street is stealing all of our money, or how the government is going to throw us all in concentration camps when we aren't looking, but I'm not. What I am going to say is that we must see that neither extreme is the way to go, because by nature, we would be far from the middle where everybody lives. I realize that people from the extremes can hold very important purposes in making the world a little better than we left it. What we need to come to terms with is, how do we know the difference?

ACTION MANIFESTO OF A MADMAN FOR GOOD

ENTRY#409

Telling the difference of how we know when the right time is for extreme sides to do something crazy, and when isn't can be difficult. We must ask ourselves, what is their goal, what is the purpose of what they want to do, have done or are saying? If their purpose is to harm as many outsiders as they can to achieve goals for their own "people" while everybody else can go to hell, than yeah it's probably not a good idea to support them. But, if their goal is to help as many people as possible so it benefits the world as a whole, than we must give a second look.

Sometimes great things can be a disguise that holds something very sinister and evil right underneath the surface waiting to strike. Sometimes the evil thing is the disguise with the great thing underneath. But sometimes there is no disguise, the truth is just out there and it is up to us what we do with it.

Knowing when extreme is too extreme or not the right time for something, is when we see a better solution that helps more people. Because that is the point of this whole thing they call life, is to help people, right?

ACTION MANIFESTO OF A MADMAN FOR GOOD

ENTRY#410

I love like I fight, with all my heart. The difference is that I see so much stronger a purpose for loving, that most of the time I choose not to fight. Does that mean that I will shy away, absolutely not. It just means that I only go after what's important. Does that mean I'm perfect, no it just means that I'm trying to figure things out like everybody else. I am no better or no worse than anybody else, and at the same time I have just as much right as they do to speak their mind, demand to be free and be given a choice.

I realize that when I have to fight I will be ready because I'll see the purpose behind it and realize there is no alternative. When does that time come, I don't know. I think people find out their own information and make their own mistakes. But if we look at everything as a lesson, then we will be able to perceive what a certain event really means.

I want everybody to know, that I love the planet and everybody in it. I love the place I'm at in my life right now, at this moment. I know that I will also be happy at the time you're reading this. How do I know, I know because I see what's really important. My eyes are open. I don't have everything figured out by far, but I do know that by being open and perceptive, I can see what I'm supposed to see and will be able to discard what I'm supposed to discard.

I don't know where I am ultimately headed in life, but I do know that I love what I see so far, and am ready for what's next.

ACTION MANIFESTO OF A MADMAN FOR GOOD

ENTRY#411

If we love ourselves and show gratitude through every action we take, than our path will shimmer in front of us. If we see that we agree more than we don't, we will see things as they actually are, not just as we would like to see them.

Whether we are talking about taxes, guns, abortion, marriage, rights of any kind or decisions of any kind, we must start from a base of gratitude and agreement. We must start talking by asking ourselves, how can we help each other out by helping each other get what we both want? We must stop arguing and start conversing. We must stop hating and start loving.

I don't want to be to set in stone. I want to be flexible enough to change presumptions I have, and nimble enough to pick up so I can learn, improve and evolve as I go.

I want to be what I need to be. And what I need to be is simple. Me.

ACTION MANIFESTO OF A MADMAN FOR GOOD

ENTRY#412

I thought by this point I would be talking about concrete solutions that would fix everything under the sun. That I would have figured out what exactly we need to do so we get past all the bullshit that we know is bullshit, and just live our true human potential. The truth is I don't have those answers; sometimes I think I wasn't supposed to. I think I was just supposed to lay the groundwork to show everybody I can that I love my life, and they can love theirs; when we do that, humanity and accountability will be second nature because any other way won't even be a question.

At this point I'm only up for what I'm supposed to do and where I'm supposed to go. Something tells me that if I slow down long enough, I will see what I am supposed to see, and learn what I am supposed to learn. I am learning and doing and being thankful. That's all of our goals, right? We all want to feel loved and feel useful, oh yeah and some of us want to make our mark. Well, what kind of mark do we want to make? Do we want to leave a stain, a crater, a mountain of garbage? Or do we want to leave more evolved than when we came in because we did our small part to keep the ball moving, and the conversation moving forward. What we do now, effects later, and vice versa. We love now, so we can love later.

ACTION MANIFESTO OF A MADMAN FOR GOOD

ENTRY#413

If what we did before effects what we do now, and what we do now effects what we do later, isn't now as a good a time as ever to start focusing on what's really important (and stop once and for all fighting the battles of the past, moving past them to a place of new understanding)?

We need to stand up and fight for what we believe in, but we also have to show love for everything that means something to us. This leads us to realize that everybody is going through the same thing and fighting and loving also. Once that thought percolates our brain for a while, we will find ourselves not wanting to step on anyone's rights because it would be like we were stepping on our own.

Will we succeed where others have failed? We will once we get past battling over who is going to take the most taxes from the most poor people. We will succeed if we stop electing politicians that act very sincere and like they want to help, but really want to take as much as they can to help out their friends. We will succeed once we realize that these politicians don't come out of nowhere. They don't get conjured up by some genie or some swami; they aren't even from another planet. They come from us; politicians will change once we change. We will always rule our own destiny as long as we allow ourselves to.

ACTION MANIFESTO OF A MADMAN FOR GOOD

ENTRY#414

We shouldn't have to put up with lies that are so apparent to anybody with eyes and half a brain, yet we do sometimes. We put up with some of the grossest negligence any person in authority or power could muster, because we don't want to make ourselves uncomfortable, or fear the awesome power that will keep us down. We must figure out what our personal trigger is, what will cause us to act.

Authenticity in character is a rare thing when it seems like lies float down like snow. Does this happen because we can't do anything about lies, we don't care or because we create them ourselves? We must find what makes us tick, what that personal thing is that makes our soul smile and say, "gee, I wish I would have found out about authenticity years ago, I finally feel free." Once we've made our discovery, we can move forward with confidence because we know we're doing it with authenticity.

So the next time there are some obvious lies thrown in our face, we can't shy away and say "it's okay, that's just the way things are and I can't do anything about it." We must stand up, point it out say, "hey, you can't get away with that. You think you can, you actually have for years but only because of the public's complacency.

Well guess what, I'm not complacent anymore. I see what you're doing, and I am not going to allow it any longer. You try to say one person can't change the world, well, what would you say if millions of people said they could and were bound to prove it?"

ACTION MANIFESTO OF A MADMAN FOR GOOD

ENTRY#415

If we would like to prove we can change the world, who are we proving it to? Are we trying to make some part of ourselves feel better, that we did something just so we can go on living our lives because we did one thing, and now we're satisfied? Are we trying to prove something to our parents that said we would never amount to anything; or because they loved us and want them to be proud of us? Are we trying to prove we can change the world to friends who say we all want to do something, but we don't know what to do?

I'm here to tell you, if you're amongst a group of friends and they say "we would all love to make positive change but we don't know what to do", tell them because we're talking about it means we know the problem exists. When we know a problem is out there, we just have to keep talking about it until a solution arises; which will work if we keep our minds on what moves us forward, not what bogs us down and takes us backward.

It's not that now is the time, (although it very well could be) the time will come when it is right. But we won't be ready for it when it does if we don't keep talking about it.

We know of the solutions and ideas that will ultimately save us, no matter what our religious or political affiliation or non-affiliation might be. We just might have to get past ourselves to get there. Can we change the world; we can if we want to. We have the solutions; the beginning is talking which is what we're already doing. The next step is to keep talking until something comes up. If the universe bends toward justice, it starts with a conversation.

ACTION MANIFESTO OF A MADMAN FOR GOOD

ENTRY#416

Gratitude is something we must feel everyday no matter what our station in life, or our tax bracket happens to be. It's something so vital to our humanity that we can't function as real human beings without it.

Somebody might say, "I'm not thankful for anything, and look at this stuff I have." I might say back, "you have money, but would you say you are a real human being that cares for the plight of all humanity"? Someone else might say, "I don't have anything and live on the street, what can I possibly be thankful for? I would reply, "Is there anything left inside you that remembers what humanity feels like, what it means to be loved and cared for?

If the people at the extremes are the problems because they can't function as real human beings, how do we help them see the metaphorical light? Is there a way they can be shown they can feel gratitude if they just give themselves a chance, a chance for their inner child to come out? We all want to love, we all want to feel love. How are we going to achieve that goal if all we spew out is hate and ugliness? How we can we hope to combat and then help out the extremes, when they're really a part of us?

We help others so we can help ourselves; we help ourselves so we can help others. Everybody helps everybody, and everybody sees how we're all interconnected. It can't be bad, if it's all good.

ACTION MANIFESTO OF A MADMAN FOR GOOD

ENTRY#417

We must be authentic people or nothing we do will have any positive effect. We mustn't lie and cheat our way to the top, because it is almost a guarantee the whole thing will crash down on top of us. We must try not to screw each other over by preventing democracy, or by blocking votes whether it's in the halls of Congress, the ballot box or the kitchen table. We must try not to intentionally hurt others, but also be always ready to defend ourselves. We must stay balanced with when to fight, when to stand up, when to compromise and when to agree.

There are a lot of things we should be doing, and a lot of things we want to do. We can get to the changes we seek when we stop doing what we've always done. We must stop trying to legislate morality, and start enforcing laws already on the books, no matter how high up the food chain the defendant is or used to be. Just because somebody is in a seat of power, doesn't mean they can just go and do whatever they want. They might think they can, which we might have lead them to believe. We must hold people in power responsible; yes that is a rule for journalists, but it should be a rule for all of us.

If we want to be an authentic person, we have to start off as ourselves, and then just be.

ACTION MANIFESTO OF A MADMAN FOR GOOD

ENTRY#418

I feel like starting a group is the best chance we have at making the change we all seek. Gathering a lot of people together and moving towards a collective goal can be a quite rewarding, but humbling experience. We all might want to make positive worldly changes, so we should get together and make them, sounds simple enough right? It sound like something we could do over a weekend with a few pizzas and some 12 packs.

Is change truly harder than what we've heard because we've proved it through experience? Even though we all know what needs to be done, do we all know what really needs to be done? Are we ready for the moment when we take back what's ours? Will there be hesitation when the bell goes off and we have to move forward?

We have to want to move forward and make positive change to make our actions effective, because if we don't, then it's not change, its stagnation, which feeds negativity. Change can be positive or negative, just like any situation we put ourselves in. We have the choice, we always have had the choice.

Should I start a group, maybe, I'm not sure yet. What I am sure of though is that I'm ready for the next great thing, the next great push in evolution that will propel us onward. Will it come from us, or some unforeseen outside source? We will never know until we open our eyes and our minds and delve into what's out there. Come on in, the water isn't getting any warmer; time to get our feet wet.

ACTION MANIFESTO OF A MADMAN FOR GOOD

ENTRY#419

The winds of change are strong, and can bowl us over at any moment; especially if we don't have an open mind and an open heart. We get confused on which way to go, as I do on a daily basis, that's what being human all is about. But we move forward anyway, because we have to figure out how to knock down our collective roadblocks. We can't just let the problem sit, festering until it gets to the point where the only solution is some very drastic measures.

We are people that make mistakes, but we learn from them, we're human. I realize not all of us have learned the lessons we have to learn yet, and if we had we might be dead. Sometimes we have to keep learning the same lesson over and over and over until it finally sinks in. We might make mistakes, but it's not that we'll never learn the lesson, there just might come a time when we have no other choice.

To feel passionate about something, we have to care for it like it's the most important thing in our lives, and we will stop at nothing to protect it. We must be caring and loving, but at the same time courageous and strong. We have to find the balance between big, strong, small and weak. We can love and be loved, while at the same time we can also be feared and hated.

We must realize not everybody is going to like us, and sometimes there's nothing we can do about it. We can't go around caring what other people think first. We must go around caring what we think first, and then others second.

Once we can think for ourselves, all our other problems will disappear.

ACTION MANIFESTO OF A MADMAN FOR GOOD

ENTRY#420

Staying open to what's out there will keep us from being dragged down, but how will we keep moving, how will we keep fighting, how will we keep loving? How can we get all our questions answered about everything right now? If life is short, then the less time we spend figuring out answers to problems, the more time we have to enjoy it right?

If good things take time, and great things happen all at once, how do we know anything will happen at all? How do we know something is great or good, if we don't have a baseline to work from? How can we hold up to the same standard as someone that enters with every advantage imaginable?

We must find our motivation. We must find our center and wash ourselves in the truth. There is something wrong when people everywhere are looking into all the most terrible possibilities, seeing every possible way they could come true. They don't seem to care about the other side of the coin, and all the good things that teamwork and partnership could produce.

If we pull back the veil on the lies we all know are there, then the system will fail. What do we do when the system fails? What if it doesn't fail, it just goes on pause for a while?

Will that be the time when we act to make a better place for us all to live? Or will we spring into action when we're just sitting there on a quiet afternoon, and all of a sudden we get a thought……

ACTION MANIFESTO OF A MADMAN FOR GOOD

ENTRY#421

I want to heal the world, I want to make change and I want to live only as long as I'm truly needed. I'm tired of trying to censor myself for everyone that can't handle a bunch of change all at once. I'm tired of those of us that say they want to make positive change, but never do. I'm tired of people that say "we can't collectively change anything because what power and influence does the little guy have?"

I'm tired of putting myself down and not allowing myself to fight and struggle so we can all live our lives in a serene and peaceful place, that isn't full of people killing and raping one another. I mean is it too much to ask that we not have banks rob us blind, while politicians and corporations hold the door open for them. Is it too much to ask that health care not come from somebody looking to screw us over at every turn, squeezing out as much money as they can. Why do we have to put up with greedy ass people that don't care about anybody except themselves?

I'm getting to the point where I will have to act, where I will have to do something that will change everything. This will be something that helps us evolve to where all the shit we've gone through for so long, won't even be a blip on the radar.

What I will do, I don't completely know yet. I do know the more open minded people we surround ourselves with, the better chance we have to make the changes that we all seek.

ACTION MANIFESTO OF A MADMAN FOR GOOD

ENTRY#422

We can be at peace if we want, we can love if we want; we can even be at the mercy of whoever is pushing our buttons and pulling our strings, if we want. We can do everything and nothing at the same time. There is choice and balance, and we must figure out how to use both of them to the best of our ability. Why must we have choice and balance to move forward? Why do we have to fight or stand up, won't somebody else do that for us so we can just continue sitting here and looking pretty?

We can feel gratitude and we can feel hate. We can feel peace, and we can feel war. We can only feel what we can feel, but at the same time, we can also change. We can also surprise ourselves by proving that we can move forward. We can unite around what we already know we agree on, because we already agree on it. We can do all the things we want to do, and be all the things that we want to be.

We have a choice. Life is constantly evolving, so we must learn to change with the times. We must not be afraid when something screams in our face that they're here to help, but we're too stubborn and stuck up to listen.

We can love each other, because we already do. We can unite with each other, because we already have. We can feel all the things that we dream of, because they are already here. Yes, we have war, famine, genocide, occupation, and as many synonyms for dehumanization as we can find, but is that because we don't stand up and say enough is enough? If you are already standing up and saying enough is enough, I commend you. You're the ones the rest of us should be following because you've taken the lead, showing us the way we can all grow together.

I love my life, and I have come to a point where I can say it and truly mean it. I wouldn't want to be in any other time or any other place than this place and this time right now. I know there is something great out there for us, we just need to go out and grab it.

ACTION MANIFESTO OF A MADMAN FOR GOOD

EPILOGUE

The biggest changes we seek start from within. All the time we spend searching for the one thing that's going to just appear and fix everything, might be better spent if we look in the mirror. We are the people we've been waiting for; we are the force that will fix everything (life is one of those things that is easy and hard at the same time). We can fix most things if we focus on what the actual problem is, and come up with solutions that include reconciliation, instead of punishment and revenge.

Politicians of any stripe have big money people in their pockets, just by the name of the game they have to procure a hefty war chest if they hope to be elected. Has it always been this way? Is this a recent development, or has it happened ever since people with money and means figured they could control the masses if they threw them some crumbs and entertained them, blinding them from what's going on behind the scenes?

We must figure out why the people with the most money always seem to have the most say, and therefore can practically buy themselves all the power and influence they want. Is it because of insecurity that they must control everything around them, and squash anybody that tries to take what they've worked for or not worked for?

Or is it because the rich have worked and struggled to move forward with their vision, and have really made something of and for themselves? Are they making money and expanding out of some want to do good, or just the aura of it? This is when we must ask ourselves whether we feel we must grab all we can, or can we see what's really important to us and the world?; the answer to why politicians screw up and screw us over could be part of the answer.

Sometimes, we as people (who walk the earth every single day) wonder when is going to be our time. When is going to be the time that we stand up and say enough is enough? When is the income gap going to be wide enough to cause a mass revolt against a machine that's designed to suck as much productivity out of its workers until they can't work anymore? Would they then just install a new one like when a battery goes dead on a new toy? The toy might stop moving and making noise, and might seem like its dead. But take the battery out and put in a new one, and the toy is like new again. The original battery is discarded, never to be thought of again because of its temporary usefulness to the user.

Why do I bring up this metaphor? Have you ever felt like an interchangeable battery that's used for what it can produce, and then discarded when something else comes along that can produce just a little bit more? The grass is always greener on the other side right, so how can we ever catch up? How are we ever going to attain what the person next to us has?

This is when we have to change our way of thinking. We must realize that there is always going to be people better and more productive than us. Some people might also be worse and way bigger slugs than us. What we have to do is work with them and not against them. We must realize we aren't in a race against the person next to us, but on a journey to make a positive impact on the world along with everybody else. Some people might think they're in a race, which is why they might need a gentle reminder that they aren't.

We're all at different places in our journey. Some of us are ready to feel the next step of evolution and understanding. Some are ready to explore where we're headed as a species and what we can do to make it the best future possible. Some of us aren't ready to think those big deep thoughts though, and are only comfortable with the simple things in life, working a job, taking care of family and hanging out with friends. We might have time for all those things, or we might not be ready, only we ourselves know the answer.

The best thing we can do is to realize everybody we've ever come into contact with, (and everybody we will come into contact with in the future) are traveling the same journey with the same basic steps as us, even though our specific lessons might be different. Once we see that everybody is going through the same things and asking themselves the same questions, (having the same basic obstacles and wanting to do the best they can) we'll see the world in a different light. I realize everybody might not appear they want to do good, but deep down they do. Maybe they've been traumatized, maybe they're selfish, whatever the reason somebody might have for not wanting to do good, only means they don't know what to do, or aren't ready. Once we realize that people are unconscious, super conscious and everything in-between, we begin to see where we're connected, where we were all once originally joined, and where we can unite again.

We might not know where we're going on a daily basis; we might not know where the end game is to the questions in life that are the biggest roadblocks we face. The best thing we can do for ourselves when we're confused and don't know what to do, is just smile. Feel gratitude for everything we have, and use that as motivation to do something positive for the rest of us that might be struggling a bit in the love department.

How do we break a violent cycle with love? How do we break a cycle of war with peace? How do we break the unending cycle of the rich getting richer and the poor getting poorer, the environment getting more polluted and developed, and the education system more gauged to making a buck than to actually teaching people? How do we break the cycle of a health care system built for making a profit instead of actual health care, or the military from running amok and killing whoever they want if it pleases the government and their aims of controlling all the means of production? How do we change a tax system so it gets the money it needs, but not the majority from people that don't have money, don't fund the government or might not even vote for them? How do you break the cycle of all that?

First, we start talking to one another. I'm not referring to talking at each other and just waiting to speak, or trying to listen while the other person is yelling that you're stupid and so are your beliefs. I'm talking about having a real conversation and sharing ideas. We can see what the other person has to say, and ask ourselves what it has to do with the place we all want to go. Will we get our chance to speak when we reach a consensus?

I think the reason this will work this time (when it hasn't so many times in the past), is that if we come from a place where we see the other person as being of the same basic makeup as us, (a member of the human race) we won't want to personally attack them because we'd be attacking ourselves.

Second, once we start talking; we can see how deep the problems go, what brought them on and what caused their growth. We can figure out what funded them, what created them, what can be done to fix them, end them, or at the very least do whatever we can so they don't happen in the future.

Third, once we realize what created generational problems at their root, we'll understand who created them, and if we had anything to do with it. Did we personally do something to cause this? Did we cause this war to break out and for people to die? Is it the way we interact with the world that brings on the major societal problems we have? When the rolling stones said in sympathy for the devil, "who killed the Kennedys, after all it was you and me," they meant it was a collective way of thinking so unaccepting of others that a person standing up to end it, was shot and killed just so we could see that we have a problem.

I love people and the earth and everyone and everything around me so much, that sometimes I don't see how people can be so harsh and so cold. Truly, how could anybody in real life be as evil as the people at the top hiding behind their curtains, and camping at their bohemian groves? They can't possibly be planning the destruction of the world because of a want to control. They must be passed the money because at the billions and trillions level it's just numbers on a computer screen anyway, so all they care about its power and influence, right? Then I remember that maybe some of these people are evil, and some aren't, I'll never know unless I know them or study them. Even then, it takes paying attention to not only what's on our sides and behind us, but most importantly what's in front of us. We must prepare to observe what the problems are, so we can get an accurate picture of how to solve them.

When we start thinking outside of the box, we start using ideas to bring us together so we can unite around what we already know we agree on. Even though we might not remember, we can have a recollection of talking and uniting when what we have in common, and how we're the same comes to the forefront of our mind instead of how we're different. We will have a good base to work from when we see that when we're fighting others, we're really fighting ourselves, and when we love others, we love ourselves. Now I ask you, would you rather love yourself, or would you rather fight and be violent and hateful to yourself?

The next step we should take is using all this knowledge we've gained from each other to fix the problems of society. It's like when we graduate college, we're supposed to go out and get a job that shows off all the things we learned, and show that all the hard work we put in wasn't a waste of time. We must go out there and use what we've learned to better humanity, and raise the consciousness of us all.

We all yearn for a better world where we can move forward and live free. We **ALL** want this, the sooner we see that, the sooner we will achieve our dreams; and the sooner we will stop trying to best other people, and start journeying alongside them.

Is the perfect world inside our head just a dream, a thought conjured up by a poor and lonely soul that had way too much time on their hands? Or is it something that we have to work at creating through our everyday actions, that weaves them throughout all our routines. We can achieve the greatness we all feel, and the greatness we all know is possible if we just got out of our own way.

We are the people that we've been waiting for, we are the souls that will heal the planet. We are the salve that will fix the wound. All the problems of the planet can be fixed if we let the fog of contention lift, and the air of truth to swirl in; "real and authentic" would be the kind of people we elect and put in power.

Sometimes there is a thought, some great philosophical point to the whole journey of life and everything that's in it (especially for this long book and the ones that preceded it). All I can say is that I'm glad I was able to put some of my thoughts out there for the masses to read. I will never stop trying to make this world a better place, my passion will never dim for humanity and my gratitude for the earth will never, ever disappear. I just want to let people know that I understand it, I get it, and I am ready to do something about it. Who is with me??

www.ingramcontent.com/pod-product-compliance
Lightning Source LLC
Chambersburg PA
CBHW030133170426
43199CB00008B/52